Fast Tracking the FAFSA

(Free Application for Federal Student Aid)

The Missing How-To Book for Financial Aid

2014-2015 Application

R J Baumel

For more tips and information about student financial aid, visit us on: www.fafsafriend.com

The chapters in this edition of the book concerning the guidance for completing the online or paper FAFSA are limited to the 2014-2015 version of the FAFSA application. Do not use these application chapters for the 2015-2016 FAFSA applications and beyond. Questions used in the FAFSA are changed, deleted or added every year. The online federal web site, FAFSA on the Web, is updated every year and data-entry screens are changed, added or deleted. Additionally, the IRS changes their tax forms every year, adding or deleting items and changing the line numbers where important income information is stored. Guidance for the 2015-2016 FAFSA will be included in next year's edition of this book; Fast Tracking the FAFSA; the Missing How-To Book for Financial Aid, the 2015-2016 Application Year Edition.

Fast Tracking the FAFSA: The Missing How-To Book for Financial Aid adheres to all regulations regarding FAFSA publications, including those outlined in the federal Higher Education Act, as amended.

Applying for financial aid does not ensure you'll receive financial aid. Federal and state laws governing financial aid programs, college policies and the information on your financial aid application will be the determining factors for financial aid eligibility.

Every effort has been made to make this book as complete as possible but no warranty or fitness is implied. The information provided is on an "as is" basis. The author and publisher shall have neither liability nor responsibility to any person or entity with respect to any loss or damages arising from the information contained in this book.

ISBN: 1492369896

ISBN 13: 9781492369899

Dedication

This book is dedicated to you, the student, whether you've already been to college or dreamed of a college education and wondered how you could get there. I wish you nothing but the best.

Acknowledgements

The very first person to thank is my editor, my sweetheart, my wife, Kathleen Povall, for all her love and support. This project would remain a glint in my eye if not for her encouragement and guidance in every step taken towards the publication of this book.

To my friends and co-editors Julie Povall and Lucy Causa Smith, for their unending and boundless energy doing all the things necessary to move the project along and for thinking of all the necessary details I keep forgetting.

And, to my children, Caitlin, Becky, Chris & Jake, for their inspiration and special place in my life.

Table of Contents

4 – Get to It and Through It: The FAFSA Online

Guidance, as needed is provided in a question-and-answer format for those choosing to complete the FAFSA via the internet at the free federal web site. Advice in this chapter helps you move from screen to screen. The screens (pages) are as follows:

5 – The Alternative: Filing The Paper FAFSA

This chapter provides question-by-question guidance for those choosing to complete the paper FAFSA application. Instructions are provided on how and where to obtain a paper FAFSA, how to complete it, and where to mail it.

6 – After The FAFSA: Read Your Mail Or E-mail

Completing the FAFSA is an important step in getting financial aid, but it's not the only step. Here, information is provided on what happens after submitting the FAFSA and what you need to do to keep the college offer of financial aid in your hands.

After completing the FAFSA, you may need to make a correction to the information on your application, such as adding another college. This chapter provides step-by-step instructions to correct or change any item on your FAFSA, whether online or by paper. The most commonly made errors are addressed with guidance for correcting them.

Many misconceptions prevent people from even applying for financial aid. This chapter reviews the most common misconceptions and clarifies the real and true information about them.

After submitting the FAFSA, there are other things you can do to make college more affordable. This chapter provides helpful tips on subjects such as finding a low cost college, how financial aid works at reducing college costs and money-saving decisions you can make after *choosing your college.*

10 – Financial Hardships or Special Circumstances: Qualifying For More Financial Aid 129

We're living in difficult financial times. If you are having a tough time, this chapter is for you. You'll find advice and step-by-step instructions to help you work with the financial aid office in order to be considered for additional financial aid.

11 – Losing My Financial Aid: It Could Happen!................137

Most student financial aid comes from government programs, and there are rules you must follow to qualify for money and to keep it. This chapter identifies the most common scenarios where a student can actually lose their financial aid after the college awards it. Advice is provided on how to avoid these slip-ups and keep the financial aid that has been awarded to you.

12 – Scholarships: How to Find Them For Free 145

This chapter provides advice on how to search for and receive scholarship financial aid from colleges and private groups and foundations without paying someone to do it.

13 – How to Save for College: The 529 Plan 155

This chapter provides advice on how to take advantage of state-sponsored 529 plans that provide tax incentives that help you save for your child's future college expenses.

Introduction
Show Me The MONEY!

This book is about having a friend in the business, the "How to Apply for Financial Aid" business. Applying for financial aid comes down to one thing - completing the FAFSA which stands for **Free Application for Federal Student Aid**.

So, why apply? The results of your FAFSA application help college financial aid offices determine what financial aid programs you qualify for as well as the amount for which you qualify. In the 2011-2012 award year there was over $200 billion in financial aid awarded nationally to those who bothered to apply for it. Over $185 billion came from the federal government alone and over 9 million students received awards from the federal Pell Grant program.

It's estimated that 28% of college-enrolled students who can qualify for financial aid do not file a financial aid application. So the question is, will you be one of the 72% of students across the country who qualifies for government aid and completes the FAFSA application process; or will you be one of the remaining 28% who qualifies, but doesn't file the application because you find it too difficult or confusing? While stories abound about how hard it is to complete the FAFSA, don't be discouraged. You really can do this with the step-by-step guidance you'll find right here in this book.

Over the years, I've made countless financial aid presentations to high school families addressing their questions about paying for college, covering topics such as types of financial aid, the federal formula for financial aid, repaying student loans, etc. But in the end, virtually every parent and student wanted to know just one thing; *tell me how to complete the FAFSA questions correctly so I can be considered for financial aid.*

"Fast Tracking the FAFSA" is here to help you get to and through the FAFSA application and in the running for some of the billions of dollars of financial aid available nationally. It's not about understanding the financial aid system, or fooling the system or finding ways to get around the system. It's really about completing and submitting the FAFSA to be *in* the system and on your way to being considered for financial aid. Keep in mind, however, that depending on the college you want to attend *and* their cost of education, you may only qualify for federal student loans. It's a common occurrence for students to qualify for different kinds of financial aid with more or less funding at different colleges.

What do you have to do to get started? The first step is to decide which approach you want to take for completing the FAFSA. There are two ways to complete the FAFSA application - online or on paper.

If you have access to a computer and can get on the internet, it's easier and faster to complete the FAFSA online. You can access the federal web site, FAFSA on the Web – Federal Student Aid, by entering **www.fafsa.ed.gov** in your browser. Instructions for completing the online FAFSA are included in Chapter 4.

If you feel more comfortable completing the paper FAFSA application, then Chapter 5 is for you. In this chapter, I will show you how to get a paper application and also give you step-by-step instructions for completing the application. Again, keep in mind that FAFSA stands for Free Application for Federal Student Aid, therefore, regardless of whether you choose to file online or on paper, the application process is free.

So, before we move on to Chapter 4 (for online applicants) or Chapter 5 (for paper applicants) you first need to know the answer to a couple of important questions.

Question #1: *Can I complete the FAFSA without including my parents' personal and income information?*

- Chapter 2 is a must-read to help you determine whether you qualify to file the FAFSA as an independent filer, (only *your* personal and financial information is needed), or a dependent filer, (you will need your parents' personal and financial information as well as your own).

Question #2: *Will I need a Federal Pin #, (an electronic signature), to complete the FAFSA?* (For online filers only)

- Please read Chapter 3 to help you determine whether you need a Federal Pin #, and if so, how to apply for one.

* * *

Chapter. 1

I Have a Question About Financial Aid....

This chapter is devoted to providing some basic, ground roots information on the subject of financial aid through a question-and-answer format. You don't need to read this chapter before you file your federal financial aid application (FAFSA), but it can help address some initial questions you may have.

What is financial aid?

There are different types of financial aid (grants, scholarships, loans and work funds) from different sources (private organizations, colleges and universities, federal and state governments). Essentially, financial aid is a discount against a college's direct expenses of tuition, fees, room and board. Financial aid can also be awarded to help you cover indirect college expenses, such as books and supplies, transportation expenses to and from your college classes and personal expenses, like lunch or a cup of coffee each day.

- Grants and Scholarships, also called gift aid, are awarded funds that do not require repayment. Scholarships are based on some form of merit, like academic merit or athletic merit and may carry renewal requirements, such as a minimum grade point average. Grants are given based on financial need as determined by filing the FAFSA, usually with no strings attached. The two major federal grant programs are;

1. The Pell grant program
2. The Supplemental Education grant program

- Loans are funds available to help you pay your college expenses, but must be repaid in the future, typically after you leave school or graduate. Some applicants may find that they qualify for only federal student loans, depending on their FAFSA information and the college's cost of education. Federal student loans have lower interest rates and a number of different repayment plans. The two major federal loan programs are;

1. The Stafford loan program
2. The Perkins loan program

- Work funds, available through the federal Work-Study Program, are opportunities for part-time jobs on-campus and off-campus. The money you earn from work study usually goes into your pocket, not the school's.

What is the Free Application for Federal Student Aid (FAFSA)?

The Free Application for Federal Student Aid (FAFSA) is the government application used to apply for federal student aid such as grants (gift aid), work-study (part-time jobs), and student loans (this money must be repaid). It is often used to qualify students for state financial aid and college financial aid programs as well. The FAFSA is the basis for determining what financial aid programs you qualify for and the dollar amount of financial aid for which you qualify.

Can I choose whether I file my FAFSA as an independent filer (without parent's information) or as a dependent filer?

No. There are questions on the FAFSA which will help you determine whether you *qualify* as a dependent or independent filer. While it used to be easier to qualify as an independent student for FAFSA purposes, widespread abuse resulted in stricter federal standards.

Is there a charge to file a FAFSA?

No. Filing your FAFSA is free. Avoid offers that charge you a fee for the FAFSA application by promising you money or scholarships in return. Whether you file the online FAFSA or paper FAFSA, the process is free.

When should my FAFSA be submitted?

For the 2014-15 academic year, submit the FAFSA anytime on or after January 1, 2014. Each college has a different deadline. Log on to each college's web site and find their financial aid application deadline. Submit your application before the earliest college deadline. If you are completing a paper FAFSA, you should mail your application no later than four weeks before the earliest deadline date. If you are filing online, submit the FAFSA by the earliest deadline. Some types of financial aid are limited and awarded to eligible students on a first-come, first-served basis.

State financial aid programs carry their own deadlines too. Go to **http:// www.fafsa.ed.gov/deadlines.htm** to see what your state deadline is and file your FAFSA early enough to meet it.

What is an Academic Year?

For traditional nonprofit colleges or universities, an academic year is the school's academic calendar of class offerings and the time of year during which they are offered. The 2014-15 academic year includes the fall 2014, the spring 2015 and the summer 2015 semesters. The FAFSA is tied to an academic year, or periods of enrollment starting after July 1, 2014, so to apply for financial aid for any of the above-mentioned semesters; you need to complete the 2014-15 FAFSA. For-profit schools that run repeating, nonstandard length programs, the 2014-15 FAFSA should be completed for periods of enrollment that begin on or after July 1, 2014 and before June 30, 2015.

Do I need to be admitted to a college before I can apply for financial aid?

No. You can submit the 2014-15 FAFSA any time after January 1, 2014. You can apply to your college(s) of choice before or after your FAFSA application date. However, to *receive* a financial aid award, you must be accepted and admitted to a college degree or certificate program (be matriculated).

How many credit hours (classes) do I have to be enrolled in to receive financial aid?

The required minimum number of credit hours varies for different types of financial aid. What I'm about to say can be different at your college, so be sure to check with them. Generally, a single college class is made up of 3 credits, or 3 hours. Half-time attendance at college is considered taking two, 3 credit classes in one semester resulting in a total of 6 credits. If you take four 3 credit college classes in a semester totaling 12 credits, you are considered a full-time student.

Every financial aid program has their own eligibility requirements designating a minimum number of classes.

1. Federal Pell grant – One class (a minimum of 3 credits) per semester
2. Federal Stafford loan – Two classes (a minimum of 6 credits) per semester
3. Some state grant programs – Four classes (a minimum of 12 credits) per semester. These requirements can vary from state to state.

Do I need to submit the FAFSA every year?

Yes. You must re-apply every year because your financial information as well as some of your personal information may change from year to year. Perhaps, the size of your family has changed, or your dependency status changed or you're attending a different college. These are just a few examples of circumstances that could affect the results of your FAFSA from year to year. Be sure to file your FAFSA each year before your college's financial aid deadline.

Are there other financial aid applications I need to complete?

That depends. Most colleges and universities across the nation only need the information from your FAFSA. Some private colleges will require a fee-based application produced by a private company. In order to be considered for additional college-based financial aid, some schools may want you to complete their institutional or college application. Some state financial aid programs have their own applications as well. Check with the college of your choice for their requirements.

What is FAFSA on the Web?

It's a federal internet application web site used by students and parents to complete the FAFSA electronically located at www.fafsa.gov .

Will I receive my FAFSA results faster if I file the application online?

Yes. Filing your FAFSA online (FAFSA on the Web) produces results faster than filing a paper FAFSA. In fact, if you file your FAFSA online and sign it with your federal PIN, you and your college(s) could receive a response approximately three to four weeks sooner than if you filed a paper FAFSA.

What is a federal PIN?

A federal PIN, which stands for Personal Identification Number, is a 4-digit number that is used in combination with your social security number, your name, and date of birth to identify you in the federal student aid databases, such as FAFSA on the Web. The federal PIN is most commonly used as an electronic signature that replaces your written signature when filing your FAFSA online. See Chapter 3 for more information.

What Information will I need to complete the FAFSA?

You will need to know your total income earned last year as well as your parents' income (if filing with a dependent status). This is the most critical information required on the FAFSA. However, bear in mind that other information you enter will also be taken into consideration, such as family size, the number of family members enrolled in college, your cash savings or investments, your high school status, your college status, marital status, citizenship or permanent resident status and whether you or your family participate in high-need federal programs. You will need to have some documents and information available to you **before** you start your FAFSA. Refer to the charts in Chapter 4 or Chapter 5 for guidance.

What if my financial circumstances have changed since I submitted the FAFSA? Can the FAFSA be changed?

If you believe that you have experienced unusual circumstances that should be taken into account, such as a significant change in income, a change of marital status (separation or divorce) or an unexpected medical expense, contact the financial aid office at the college you plan to attend. They can help you readjust your FAFSA information to reflect this change. Do not try to make this kind of adjustment yourself on your FAFSA. Please reference Chapter 10.

Who decides how much financial aid I will receive and what types of financial aid I will receive?

The financial aid offices of the college(s) you apply to will review your completed FAFSA to determine your eligibility for different financial aid programs. They will determine what types of financial aid (grants, loans, work-study) you qualify for and the dollar amount for each category. Your awards can vary from college to college.

How will I receive my financial aid?

Your financial aid will be applied to your college student account to help pay your direct charges of tuition, fees, and room and board for the term(s) you're enrolled in. If there is financial aid money left over after your direct costs are covered, your college must give you a cash refund for that amount.

Can I receive financial aid if I am not a U.S. citizen?

Yes. There are noncitizen visa status designations that qualify for federal and state financial aid programs. If you're neither a citizen nor eligible noncitizen, it is possible that you may still qualify for institutional (college) money. If this situation applies to you, call the financial aid office of the college you want to attend to find out.

I don't want my personal and private information to be shared. Do all the agencies of the federal government and all departments of the colleges to which I've applied have access to my information?

No. With the exception of the U.S. Department of Education, which is the federal department to which the FAFSA's are submitted, federal privacy laws protect the information you provide on the FAFSA. Other agencies including the IRS, CIA, FBI, state police, news organizations as well as most other departments of any college you apply to *cannot* view your private information without your expressed, written permission or a court order.

If I provide information for my child on the FAFSA, I'll be forced to pay for my child's education, right?

Wrong. Providing information as a parent for your child on the FAFSA in no way legally requires the parent to pay even one red cent (or copper penny either). The information you provide will determine your eligibility for financial aid…that's all.

I'm a graduate student, attending school to complete a master's or doctoral degree program. Can I qualify for federal and/or state grants?

No. Federal grants, and in most cases state grant financial aid programs, are limited to students in undergraduate programs, such as those students pursuing associate or bachelor's degrees or certificates. However, many colleges offer fellowships and assistantships to graduate students enrolled on master's or doctoral programs as a means to attract and retain students at their institution. Contact your financial aid office for information regarding these funding opportunities.

For the purpose of completing the FAFSA, who is defined as a parent?

A parent is defined as a biological parent or adoptive parent. A step-parent's information cannot be used to complete the FAFSA <u>unless</u> he/she is legally married to the biological or adoptive parent. Legal guardians, such as uncles, aunts, grandparents, etc., do not fall under the definition of a parent. Therefore, their information cannot be included in your FAFSA. You may qualify as an independent student. Refer to Chapter 2 to determine if you qualify.

* * *

Chapter. 2

Can I Complete The FAFSA Without My Parents' Information?

Are You A Dependent or Independent FAFSA Filer?

This chapter will help you determine if you (the student) can complete the FAFSA without reporting your parents' personal and financial information. It's important to note that your dependency status is not simply a personal choice. It's a status you qualify for by answering "Yes" or "No" to a series of 13 questions found in the dependency section of the FAFSA.

So before completing the 2014-2015 FAFSA, review the questions in the chart on the following page to determine if you are a dependent or independent FAFSA filer. This checklist will help you determine if your parents' information is needed to complete your FAFSA.

		YES	NO
1.	Were you born before January 1, 1991?		
2.	During the school year 2014-15, will you be working on a master's or doctorate program (such as a MA, MBA, MD, JD, PhD, EdD, or graduate certificate, etc.?		
3.	As of today, are you married? (Answer "YES" if you are separated, but not divorced.)		
4.	Do you have children who receive more than half of their support from you between July 1, 2014 and June 30, 2015?		
5.	Do you have dependents (other than your children or spouse) who live with you and who receive more than half of their support from you, now and through June 30, 2015? *This question asks if you're supporting your parents, grandparents, or other types of family members.*		
6.	At any time since you turned 13, were both your parents deceased or were you in foster care or were you a ward of the court? *This question refers to a court action that has determined your status as a "ward of the court".*		
7.	Are you a veteran of the U.S. Armed Forces, honorably discharged?		
8.	Are you currently serving on active duty in the U.S. Armed Services for purposes other than training? **National Guard counts ONLY if members are placed on active duty.*		
9.	Are you or were you an emancipated minor as determined by a court in your state of legal residence? (A copy of the court decision may be requested by your financial aid office.) **The key word here is "court", as in **court-ordered**. Your decision to separate from your parent(s) and go off on your own does not apply here.*		
10.	Are you or were you in legal guardianship as determined by a court in your state of legal residence? (A copy of the court decision may be requested by your financial aid office.) **The key word here is "court", as in **court-ordered**. Your parents are NOT your legal guardians for the purpose of completing the FAFSA. Also, you are NOT a legal guardian of yourself*		
11.	At any time on or after July 1, 2013, did your high school or school district homeless liaison determine that you were an unaccompanied youth who was homeless?		
12.	At any time on or after July 1, 2013, did the director of an emergency shelter or transitional housing program (funded by the federal government) determine that you were an unaccompanied youth who was homeless?		
13.	At any time on or after July 1, 2013, did the director of a runaway or homeless youth basic center or transitional living program determine that you were an unaccompanied youth who was homeless or were self-supporting and at risk of being homeless?		

For questions 11 through 13, use the following definitions:

(The word "**unaccompanied**" means you are not living in the physical custody of your parent(s) or guardian(s). "**Youth**" means that you are 21 years of age or younger, "**homeless**" means lacking fixed, regular or adequate housing, as in living in a shelter, motel, car, tent, etc.).

If you answered "YES" to *at least one question*, then you are considered an **independent filer**. If you answered "NO" to *every question*, then you are considered a **dependent filer** and you must complete both the student and parent information on the FAFSA.

Now that you know what dependency status you qualify for, you are ready to go to Chapter 3 to acquire your federal PIN (skip this chapter if you are completing a paper FAFSA). Afterwards, head to either Chapter 4 and begin the FAFSA online process or Chapter 5 to complete the paper FAFSA.

If you answered "NO" to every question, but believe that there are special circumstances that might qualify you as an independent filer, contact your financial aid office for clarification and assistance.

* * *

Chapter. 3

Get Your Federal PIN: Signing The FAFSA Online

Believe me, if you want to use the internet to electronically file your FAFSA, this is where it starts. This chapter is only a few pages, so do yourself a big favor and read it.

A federal PIN is an electronic signature used to sign your completed online FAFSA. This same federal PIN, which personally identifies you, will be used every year you complete the FAFSA online; so remember it, write it down and keep it in a safe place. Not only will you use it to submit the FAFSA, but you will use it after submission to make corrections and check on the status of your application. When you want to access your information on the federal database, your PIN tells this secure site *"Hey, this is really me. Please show me my personal information on this site."*

By now you've read Chapter 2 and have determined whether you qualify to apply as a dependent student or an independent student. If you are filing as an independent student and completing the FAFSA with only your information (plus your spouse's, if married), then you only need a federal PIN for yourself. However, if you are filing as a dependent student, you, as well as one parent, will each have to apply for a federal PIN. Please note that if the parent who is signing your FAFSA does not have a social security number, he/she cannot obtain a federal PIN and cannot sign your FAFSA electronically. In this case, print out the signature page at the end of the FAFSA, have your parent sign it, and mail it to the address indicated.

You can have the web site assign a federal PIN to you or you will have the option of creating one for yourself. Since you will use it and reuse it, treat it like any other personal password you have for your e-mail or social networking sites. *Don't forget it* or forget where you put it for safe keeping and don't give it out to anyone! Let me say this again…don't give your pin out to anyone!! Even if someone is helping you fill out the online FAFSA, do not reveal your federal PIN. It's on a need-to-know basis, and they don't need to know.

To ensure the security of this PIN, you will be asked to choose a challenge question from a group of questions provided in a drop-down menu. Choose a question you can easily answer. You will then be asked to provide the answer to that question. Why this extra step, you ask? If you ever forget your password or have to request a new PIN, website security will ask you this question to be sure it is actually you; and you will be expected to provide the exact answer you gave when you first set up your PIN.

Here's good news! After your first year's FAFSA is filed, future applications should become less time consuming. When you sign into the website with your PIN the following year, you will be asked if you would like to carry over certain information from last year's FAFSA (called a Renewal FAFSA). If you choose to do this, you will have an opportunity to review this information for accuracy and then move on to entering the current year's financial information.

Where do you go online to get a federal PIN? To get a federal PIN, go to **www.pin.ed.gov** or click on "PIN Site" on the menu bar of FAFSA online at **www.fafsa.gov**. Either one of these links will get you to the PIN site.

Regardless of which way you choose to access this website, the screen in front of you should contain the following.

You will see the federal tree logo in the left corner of the screen and in the middle top portion will be the message;

"Welcome to the Federal Student Aid"
PIN Web Site

On the left of the screen is a light blue area containing a menu of possible actions, such as applying for a PIN for the first time or, recovering your PIN if you forgot it. The menu options are:

- Apply for a PIN
- Check PIN Status
- Request a Duplicate PIN
- Access my PIN E-Mail
- Change my PIN
- Update my Personal Information
- Disable my PIN
- Re-establish my PIN
- Activate my PIN

If you are applying for a PIN for the first time, you can also click on the blue "Apply Now" button in the box in the lower right side of the screen.

If this is the first time you are applying for a PIN, do the following;

- You can either click on "Apply for A PIN" in the blue highlighted menu on the left side of the screen or on the blue "Apply Now" button in the box on the right side of your screen.

- You will then be given some basic information on applying for a PIN. Click "NEXT" to continue.

- You will be asked to enter some personal information including your name. *Be sure to enter your name exactly as it appears on your social security card.* You will also enter your current address and your social security number.

- There are two additional questions that follow that allow you to create your own personal PIN. You can skip these questions if you want the web site to automatically assign you a PIN. After all the questions are answered click "NEXT". There's your PIN!

Once you have a PIN do you ever have to apply for one again? No, the same PIN can be used for every year you file a FAFSA, which is every year you are attending school and filing for financial aid.

If you have forgotten your PIN, follow the steps below;

- Click on the third item in the blue highlighted menu to the left of the screen, "Request a Duplicate PIN" and fill in the requested items. Then click on "Submit Request".

- You'll be brought to the page that asks you the challenge question you previously chose when you originally applied for your PIN. Enter your answer to the challenge question and hit "Submit Request" again.

- You'll see information about yourself. If it's correct, select how you'd like to receive your PIN. You can have it displayed immediately on the screen or you can request to have it sent to you via the postal service or e-mailed to you. If you want the PIN on screen, select "Display Now" and click "Submit Request" once more. There's your PIN! Write it down or print out the page for future reference.

If you think that someone else may know your PIN, or you believe your PIN has been made public in any way, you can get a new PIN and have it sent to you by postal service or electronically by e-mail. To submit a request for a new PIN, select "Change My PIN" from the menu on the left of the PIN web page and go on from there.

$$* * *$$

Chapter. 4

Get To It and Through It:
The FAFSA Online

*(Note: Skip this chapter if you're filing
your FAFSA by paper)*

C ompleting the FAFSA application at the federal web site, called
FAFSA on the Web – Federal Student Aid, can take as few as 22
minutes, down from an average of 33 minutes last year.

Of the 22 million applicants that filed the FAFSA last year, about 99%
completed the application online. Why? Because it's a user-friendly
site with technology that can shorten the application completion time
while offering helpful tips and guidance throughout the process. For
those whose language preference is Spanish, the entire website is easily
translated from English into Spanish by clicking a button featured on the
home page.

The FAFSA on the Web process is very intuitive. The software will take you to the next set of questions based on your answers to previous questions. As a result, unnecessary questions are skipped and never displayed for you to complete. This process also checks your application for errors and omissions as you complete each section, making the application process quick and easy. You'll find that there's helpful information on each internet page in the "Help and Hints" box for every item you'll need to complete. You can also click "NEED HELP?" on the bottom of each screen. With that said, in my years of experience helping online filers like yourself, I've found that just about everyone gets stuck somewhere along the way. So, I've organized this chapter in a question-and-answer format (FAQ) for every section and FAFSA page (screen). These are questions students have asked me as they've tried to complete their FAFSA. If you get stuck, go to the corresponding FAFSA page (screen) in this chapter and look for the answer to your question.

Before you begin, please check the chart below for important personal documents you should have on hand to ensure that you complete the application with accuracy.

DOCUMENT	Dependent Filer		Independent Filer	
	Student	Parent(s)	Student	Spouse
Social Security Card (Original or Copy) * You (the student) must have a valid social security number	✓	✓	✓	
State issued Drivers' License (if you have one)	✓		✓	
2013 Federal Income Tax Return (no state returns)	✓	✓	✓	✓
2013 Non-Taxable Income Information such as child support (not alimony), pension contributions, veteran's non-educational benefits such as disability, death pension, dependency compensation, etc. You can find this information on veterans benefit letters, court documents, etc.	✓	✓	✓	✓
2013 W-2 Forms (if any) received from employer(s)	✓	✓	✓	✓
Asset Information such as bank accounts, investments, real estate, business and farms.	✓	✓	✓	✓

The Basics:

- Computer and Internet Access:

You'll need a computer with access to the internet and an up-to-date internet browser. If you don't have a computer or internet access at home, don't worry. Many libraries, high schools, and local colleges have computer rooms or labs that have computers available for public use. Just be careful who's looking over your shoulder while you're doing the FAFSA and make sure, *really make sure,* that you close the browser session on the public computer after you're done so that the next person can't see your personal information.

- Eligibility:

Are you eligible for financial aid? To be eligible for federal or state financial aid, grants, loans, or work study, you must be a U.S. citizen or an eligible noncitizen (permanent resident). If you are neither of these, there are still other immigration statuses that can make you eligible for financial aid such as an I-551C Conditional Immigration Status; certain I-94 designations; if you are a Canadian born Native American; or are a resident of certain U.S. territories. If none of these apply to you, close your internet browser and call your college financial aid office. You still may be considered for financial aid. You also must be enrolled in an eligible academic program, not be in default on a previous student loan, and demonstrate financial need.

- Know your deadlines:

This is very important! Financial aid deadlines for filing the FAFSA vary from school to school. After you've decided which colleges you want to include on your FAFSA, log on to each college's web site and find their financial aid application deadline. Write down the deadlines for each of these schools. Which one of these schools has the earliest deadline? You should file your online FAFSA no later than that day (the day of the earliest deadline). Submitting the FAFSA after a college's financial aid deadline could result in not being considered for some of their financial aid programs. Additionally, state financial aid programs carry their own application deadlines as well. Be prepared for that.

Go to **http://www.fafsa.ed.gov/deadlines.htm** to see what your state deadline is and file your FAFSA early enough to meet it.

As a side note, do not confuse college admissions deadlines with FAFSA submission deadlines. They are two totally different deadlines.

- "You", means you, the student:
Parents, this is not your application, so when the FAFSA has the word "you" or "your" in any sentence or question; they are referring to "the student".

- One last word:
There are no guarantees in life and no guarantees here either. Consider the art of fishing. You toss your line out, but you have no certainties that you'll pull in that trophy fish. You're applying for financial aid, but there are no certainties you'll receive financial aid, grants, student loans or part-time jobs. How your college's financial aid office determines your eligibility for awarding will depend on a number of factors including the information you include on your FAFSA, when you submit the FAFSA (less money is available if you file after the deadline), the amount of financial aid funds the college has available, whether you are enrolled in an eligible academic program, and other considerations. Keep in mind that depending on the college you want to attend and their cost of education, you may not qualify for any financial aid or only qualify for federal student loans.

Screen Navigation Tip:

Like other government web pages, you need to be careful how you move back and forth from screen to screen or you'll get booted out. *Don't* use the navigation arrows in the left corner of your internet screen. Check out the bottom of your screen. *Use* the "PREVIOUS" and "NEXT" buttons to go back and forth from screen to screen. Also, on the bottom of the screen is where the "SAVE" Button lives. I recommend that you save your application information on every other FAFSA page so you don't lose your entered information if your internet connection drops. Do this, *really*. It's the internet and you can be dropped from a site at any time!

Federal privacy laws protect the information you provide on the FAFSA from prying eyes. Other federal or state agencies, including the IRS, FBI, Homeland Security, state police, etc. *cannot* view your private information without your expressed, written permission, or a court order.

As we begin, keep in mind that you should only enter whole dollar amounts in every money question. Even if your tax return shows a figure in dollars and cents, round up or down to the nearest whole dollar.

Fire-up your computer internet browser and go to FAFSA on the web, located at: HTTPS://www.fafsa.gov. (make sure the ending is ".**gov**").

The URL address you typed in should bring you to the home page of FAFSA on the Web. The term "**Federal Student Aid**", located in the upper left corner of your screen, is an office in The U.S. Department of Education. The slogan for this web site, as follows…

"Get Help Paying for College" is in a blue bar at the top.

Under the pictures of a few smiling students are two choices for starting a FAFSA:

- "**New to the FAFSA?**" (Start here if you are a new FAFSA filer.)

- "**Returning User?**" (Start here if you are someone who filed a FAFSA previously.) In this section, students can make corrections to a previously submitted FAFSA, add a school, and view information on their Student Aid Report (SAR) which is issued after the FAFSA is submitted. See Chapter 6 for more information on the SAR.

Underneath each of these choices is a green button to begin the FAFSA process. This is where it all begins…Now, click the green button, "Start a New FAFSA" or click the green "Login" button as a returning user and sign in at the Login page.

Login page: Student Information
Frequently asked questions for this page:

Visual Aid:

Let's look around the Login page and get comfortable. Check out the right side of your screen. Do you see the "Help and Hints" box? Every time you click into a question field, detailed help appears for every question in this box; so, keep an eye out for this feature. It can be very helpful and quicken your pace. See the blue bar on the left? That bar will show either "STUDENT" or "PARENT" on each screen page so you know whose information to enter.

Q: Why do I need my social security card to put in my name and social security number?

> **A:** You must enter your legal name and social security number *exactly* as it appears on you card. The federal processor matches your exact name and social security number with the Social Security Administration to confirm that you are a citizen. This information is also used to confirm your residency status with the Department of Homeland Security if you are a permanent resident. One incorrect letter or number will negate this electronic match.

Q: I changed my name because I got married/divorced and it's different from my social security card. What name do I use?

> **A:** You must enter your name and social security number *exactly* as it appears on you social security card. The federal processor checks this information with the Social Security Administration or Homeland Security to confirm your citizenship. Go to your social security office if you want your name changed.

Q: My name is different on my citizenship certificate or my alien registration card in comparison to my social security card. What name do I use?

A: You must enter your name and social security number *exactly* as it appears on your social security card because the federal processor checks this information with the Social Security Administration or Homeland Security to confirm your citizenship or permanent residency status. Go to the Social Security office if you want your name changed.

Q: How do I know whose information to put in; student or parent?

A: Do you see the blue bar on the left of your screen? That bar will show either "STUDENT" or "PARENT" on each screen so you know whose information to enter.

Q: Where can I get help for any items appearing on these FAFSA pages?

A: Check out the right side of the screen you're on. Do you see the "Help and Hints" box? Every time you click into a question field, detailed help appears for every question in this box. You can also click on the "NEED HELP?" button on the bottom of the screen. You can also call the federal hotline at 1.800.433.3243.

Get Started page
Frequently asked questions for this page:

Q: Which FAFSA application should I choose; the 2013-2014 or the 2014-2015 application?

A: Up until June 30, 2014, you can still apply for financial aid for the 2013-14 academic year, which applies to classes scheduled to run no later than June 30, 2014. Afterwards, only the 2014-2015 FAFSA will be available for you to complete. Essentially, for any academic program beginning on or after July 1, 2014 (that includes attending classes beginning

September, 2014 or January, 2015), you should complete the 2014-2015 FAFSA.

MY FAFSA page
Frequently asked questions for this page:

Q: What is a Renewal FAFSA?

A: A renewal FAFSA gives a returning student the option of using information from last year's FAFSA and copying it into the current year's FAFSA automatically. This is a time-saving feature when doing your FAFSA online. A number of informational items from a previously completed FAFSA can be used to populate your 2014-15 FAFSA saving you time and effort. Make sure you glance over the information copied into your FAFSA to ensure it's accurate.

Q: What is a federal PIN?

A: A federal PIN (Personal Identification Number) is the tool you need to sign your FAFSA electronically. You have the option to print out a signature page, sign it and mail it to the federal processor after you submit your FAFSA online. However, it will delay the processing of your FAFSA for weeks. Remember, if you need your parents' information to complete the FAFSA, one of your parents will need to get a PIN as well. This parent must have a valid social security number to obtain their PIN. Please refer to Chapter 3 to learn more about the PIN and how to get one.

Start Your 2014-2015 FAFSA page
Frequently asked questions for this page:

Q: Why do I need to create a password here?

A: If you decide to take a break from completing the FAFSA, and close down your internet session, you can come back to it at a later time with the password you're creating now. All your previous work will be saved (by pressing the "SAVE" button before you close down) and be right where you left it. Don't wait longer than 45 days, however. After 45 days, incomplete applications are deleted from the federal database.

INTRODUCTION PAGE – 2014-2015 FAFSA
This page contains helpful information on various parts of the FAFSA application. You can gather some information before you're ready to proceed. Click the "NEXT" button to continue.

Student Demographic Information page
Frequently asked questions for this page:

Q: Can I skip a question as I go through the FAFSA online process?

A: There are some items you'll find you can skip and some that you can't. The web site will stop you from proceeding and provide red-colored warning messages for those items you need to answer. Check the "Help & Hints" box for more information or go to the FAFSA page help provided in this chapter for additional guidance.

Q: Should I save my information as I go through the FAFSA online process?

A: Yes, absolutely. Sometimes, while on the internet, a spike occurs or you're dropped from the web site for no apparent reason. When this happens, any information you did not save will be lost. Preserve your information while completing your FAFSA by pressing the "SAVE" button on the bottom of each screen.

Q: My name, birth date and social security number are already filled in on this page but other items are blank. Should I fill in these remaining items?

A: Yes, you need to complete all items that apply to you on this page. Your name, birth date and social security number carried over from your login page information and were filled in automatically.

Q: I might be moving soon, what address do I enter?

A: If you think you might be moving in the future, enter your current mailing address. If you move later on, file a change of address form with your post office. Your mail will follow you for up to a year. Oh, and let the college Registrar know your new address too. Hey, cover all the bases.

Q: What if I answer "No" to the state residency question that asks if I lived in my state since 2009? Will that prevent me from getting financial aid?

A: No. I'm not aware of any state that requires you to live there for 5 years to be a state resident. Furthermore, your eligibility for federal financial aid is *not affected* by your answer about state residency. Most states only require that you and at least one parent (dependent filers) are residents of your state for a full year before you start attending your college. If you are an independent filer, only your residency matters. There is considerable financial aid that is offered from many states across the country and qualifying for funds depends on each state's definition of a legal resident. Check with your college about residency requirements for financial aid.

Q: I'm not sure what marital status to enter because it's changing soon. What do I do?

A: Enter your marital status *as of the day you complete and submit the FAFSA*. Select "single" if you are not married. If you are married, separated, or divorced, another question box appears underneath that asks you for the date this status occurred. *Please note;* if your marriage is termed "same-sex", and you were legally married in the 14+ states (or in the District of Columbia) that permit same-sex marriages, you must include your spouse's information on the FAFSA. You will be considered "married" for this application. This is also the case if your parents are a same-sex couple who are legally married and completing this FAFSA with you.

Another change for 2014-15 requires information from both legal parents (biological or adoptive) who are living together. Information and incomes for both of these parents must be reported, regardless of whether they are legally married or not under federal law.

Q: I'm not married but live with my girlfriend/boyfriend. Should I include my girlfriend/boyfriend's information in my application?

A: No, since you are not legally married, only the applicant's information is required. However, you may need to report any financial support you receive for living expenses as non-taxable income.

Q: My uncle claims me on his federal tax return, but I live on my own and qualify as an independent student. Whose information should I include; my uncle's and/or my own?

A: If you qualify as an independent student, you should only include *your* information on your FAFSA. The fact that your uncle claimed you on his tax return has no bearing on your FAFSA.

Q: I am married and we are a same-sex couple, legally married in a state permitting same-sex marriages. Should I include my spouse's information in my FAFSA?

A: Yes, include your spouse's information in your FAFSA. Federal law now recognizes legal same-sex marriages. This is a new change for the 2014-15 filing year.

Q: Is it important to provide my e-mail address?

> **A:** It is important. Read the Help and Hints section on the right side of the screen regarding e-mail addresses. Your e-mail address allows the federal processor to send you an e-mail notification regarding your FAFSA application.

Q: I'm going to get married soon. Should I wait to complete my financial aid application?

> **A:** Not necessarily. Some students actually receive more financial aid filing as a dependent filer. If you wait, you will have to include your spouse's income as well as your own. Furthermore, independent, married students without dependents are treated more harshly in the federal needs analysis formula than dependent students or married students with dependents.

Student Eligibility page
Frequently asked questions for this page:

Q: Why is this page showing a field requiring me to enter an alien registration number?

> **A:** In the question regarding citizenship, you indicated that you are an eligible noncitizen, or permanent resident. As a result, an alien registration number from a citizenship document called an alien registration or "green card" is required. If you are a U.S. citizen, go back and change your answer to "U.S. citizen".

Q: I am neither a U.S. citizen nor eligible noncitizen, how does that affect my qualifying for financial aid?

> **A:** You can complete the rest of the FAFSA, but your eligibility for financial aid is in question. Call your financial aid office for guidance. Remember, there are a number of immigration statuses that qualify.

Q: What is Selective Service?

A: Selective Service registration is required of most males between 18 and 26 years of age. It was put in place for the U.S. Army draft, but that ended long ago. The requirement to register is still a necessity to qualify for federal funds. If you entered "female" to the gender question on the previous Student Demographic Information page, or you are over 26 years of age, you will not be shown this question. If you select "No" (not registered), and you're male and you are past your 18th birthday, you should check the "Register Me" box for automatic registration with Selective Service. If, however, you are male, over 26 years of age and never registered, you will need to submit information to the college financial aid office regarding why you did not meet this requirement. You cannot receive financial aid until the financial aid office reviews this information.

Q: I am a high school student that hasn't graduated yet. What high school status do I indicate?

A: The question starts with the phrase "When you begin college in the 2014-15 school year". So, indicate your high school completion status (high school graduate, GED, home-schooled, etc.) as of the day you will start attending college. You must be a high school graduate, have a GED, or be certified by your state as home-schooled to be eligible for financial aid.

Q: Why would I be interested in federal Work Study?

A: The federal Work Study program provides part-time, on-campus and off-campus job opportunities. I recommend saying "yes", no matter what. It doesn't obligate you to accept a job, but it keeps your options open. However, most work study payments are directed to you, the student, and not toward your tuition and fees.

Q: Is the question about a bachelor's degree asking if I want a bachelor's degree or if I already have one?

A: Read this one carefully. This question doesn't ask if you *want* a bachelor's degree (BA) right now. It is asking if you *have earned* one by July 1, 2014. It also doesn't matter if the degree was earned domestically or in a foreign country.

Q: What grade level do I enter if I've already completed a bachelor's degree and I'm going for an associate's degree or another bachelor's degree?

A: Do not enter "1st Year Graduate/Professional" or "Continuing Graduate/Professional or Beyond" for this question. Enter an undergraduate grade level (freshman, sophomore, junior or senior). In general, if you have a bachelor's degree *and* transfer your credits earned from your previous school, you can estimate your level as being a junior. If you are entering a community college, *and* transfer your credits earned from your previous school, you can estimate your grade level as being a sophomore.

Q: I'm seeing questions about whether I have a drug conviction. Why am I seeing these questions?

A: This question arises if you said "Yes" to the question about receiving financial aid in the past. This question is attempting to determine if you had a drug conviction *while you received federal financial aid*, making you initially ineligible to receive funding. If you have been convicted of a drug offense *while receiving* financial aid, save and close your application and contact the financial aid office. They may be able to assist you in regaining your financial aid eligibility. If you are entering college for the first time, you will not see this question.

Student Eligibility Continued page
Frequently asked questions for this page:

Q: I entered the name, city and state of my high school and clicked the "CONFIRM" button, but my high school didn't appear in the list. Is this a problem? What do I do now?

> **A:** If you don't see your high school listed, check the address you entered and try clicking the "CONFIRM" button again. If you still don't see your high school, you may have to correct it later or provide proof to the financial aid office that you have a high school diploma or GED. This is a fairly new field. The federal U.S. Department of Education is compiling a list of high schools across the country and it's not complete yet. Click the "NEXT" button to continue.

Q: I attended a foreign high school. Will this prevent me from getting financial aid?

> **A:** No. If your high school from your home country is not listed when you search for it, this is of no concern and will not prevent you from qualifying for financial aid, as long as you are a high school graduate and meet the citizenship requirements.

Q: I didn't see a question asking me about the name of my high school. Do I need to go back a screen or two to find it?

> **A:** No, you may not need to answer this question, based on the information you already provided on your FAFSA. Only those applicants who have never attended college previously or attended for one or two years will be asked this question. If you are an upperclassman undergraduate (junior or senior) or a graduate student, you will not see this question.

School Selection page
Frequently asked questions for this page:

Q: Why do I need to select a college?

A: The college(s) you select here will receive your completed FAFSA. This is important because each individual college you apply to determines their financial aid offer based on the information you include in your FAFSA. You have to include at least one college.

Q: Do I have to wait to be accepted into a college before I select the college on my FAFSA application?

A: No, you can apply for financial aid for any college before, during, or after you apply to the college or before or after you're accepted for admissions. Don't wait. And remember to meet the college's financial aid deadline.

Q: If I'm not sure what college I want to attend, can I skip this FAFSA page? What do I do?

A: No, the web site requires that you enter at least one college. If you're not sure, pick one or enter all your college choices, up to a maximum of ten. You can always go back after you've submitted your FAFSA and change or add colleges you want. Remember, it's free.

Q: What is a federal school code? Do I need this code to find and select the school I want my FAFSA to go to?

A: The federal school code is a unique six-digit number assigned to every college for the FAFSA process. While having the federal school code makes for an easier search, you don't need it to find your college. You can search for any college on this screen by entering the college name and the city and state where it's located. Once you find it on the list (scroll down the screen), click the box on the left of the college name and click the "ADD" button. Be careful to select the right college. Some colleges have the same name so be sure to check the address and state of your college.

Q: What if I'm not sure if I'm going to live with my parents, in the dormitories or off-campus in an apartment? What do I do?

A: You must select one of the options now, but you can change it later after the FAFSA is submitted or by letting the college financial aid office know of your change. Changing your mind about your living arrangements is something many students do in the course of attending college. If you are still unsure, select "living on campus" and change your status with the financial aid office later on.

Dependency Determination page
Frequently asked questions for this page:

Q: I want to file my FAFSA without my parents' information. Why am I being asked these questions?

A: Filing your FAFSA as an independent filer is not your choice. You must *qualify* for this status, based on legal requirements set for the FAFSA. The questions on this page are designed to determine if you are independent or dependent (need parents' information) for the purpose of completing this FAFSA. These are the questions you reviewed in Chapter 2. Dependent applicants must provide parent information, in most cases. If you feel you can't provide parent data, read the next question.

Q: There's a message on this screen indicating that I'm dependent, but I can skip parents' information if I have a special circumstance. What does that mean?

A: For dependent students, a special circumstance is a situation that exists between the student applicant and his or her parent(s) which prevents the student from providing parental information. For example, your parents are incarcerated, or you left home due to an abusive family situation, or you do not know where your parents are and are unable to contact them. If you think a special circumstance might apply to you, save your application, close your browser, and contact your college financial aid office.

Q: I don't live with my parents. Why am I being told that I'm dependent and must provide my parents' information?

A: It may appear that you are independent and self-supporting by living on your own, but this doesn't qualify you as an independent filer for financial aid purposes, unless you are an emancipated minor determined by a court in your state. Otherwise, you need to include parent information.

Q: There's a message on this screen indicating that I qualify as independent, but I live with my parents. Did I do something wrong?

A: No. You may qualify as an independent filer for a number of reasons and still be living with your parents. For example, if you were born before January 1, 1991, or you're a veteran of the armed forces, or you are supporting a child, you qualify as an independent filer and are not required to enter parent information, even if you live with your parents.

Q: I live with parents or friends or relatives and this FAFSA process determined that I'm an independent filer. Do I include these people in my household size?

A: No. You do not include parents, friends, aunts, uncles, etc. in your household size. If your marital status is single, put in a household size of "1". In this case, you should also enter "1" to the question asking "How many people in your household will be attending college?"

Q: What is an emancipated minor?

A: An emancipated minor is a court-ordered determination in the state where you reside that establishes you as independent or in legal guardianship. The court order cannot be the result of a divorce agreement.

Q: What is an unaccompanied youth?

A: The word "**unaccompanied**" for financial aid purposes means you are not living in the physical custody of your parents or guardian. The word "**youth**" means that you are 21 years of age or younger.

Q: This FAFSA page indicates that I can file as independent without my parents' information, but there's a question asking me if I want to put in parent information. Should I?

A: Independent applicants can say "NO" to answer parent questions without affecting their eligibility for federal and state financial aid. Check with your college if they require parental information for college-awarded financial aid.

Q: What if I need my parents' information, but can't get it?

A: There may be reasons why you can't get your parents to cooperate and help you process the FAFSA. Perhaps they do not want to share their personal financial information, or perhaps they do not want to contribute to your education. You can continue as a dependent filer and complete the FAFSA without parent information, but you will only qualify for a federal unsubsidized student loan. To be considered for more financial aid, particularly grants, you need to contact your college financial aid office and they can help you determine what you need to do.

> **Screen Navigation Tip:**
>
> Important: If you answered "Married" to the marital status question in the Student Demographic Page (i.e.; you're married), or your date of birth is *on or before* January 1, 1991, many of the 13 questions in this section will not appear (Isn't that cool?) because the FAFSA has already determined that you are an independent filer. You'll answer questions about your household size and number of household members attending college. Afterwards, you'll be brought automatically to the Student Tax Information Page.
>
> If the FAFSA web site determined you to be a dependent filer, you'll continue on with parent basic information.

Parent Demographic page
Frequently asked questions for this page:

Q: How do I decide which parent to include on my FAFSA?

> **A:** Generally speaking, the parent you live with is the one completing the FAFSA with you. If you live with your mom and dad, or a parent and a step-parent, both of their personal and financial information should be included. If you live with only one parent, then the parent you live with should be included in your FAFSA, even if the other parent claims you on his/her tax return. Please note that if the one parent you live with is a step-parent, you cannot include their information on your FAFSA. A step-parent is a valid parent *only* when married to your biological or adoptive parent. If you don't live with your parents, you may choose the parent who gives you the most financial support or contact your financial aid office to discuss your personal situation.
>
> If you don't live with your parents, but live with legal guardians or others such as aunts, uncles, brothers, sisters, etc., they do not fit the definition of a parent for FAFSA purposes. The financial aid office may decide to have you file as an independent student, if you meet certain conditions.

Q: Why is the FAFSA referring to my parents as "parent 1" and "parent 2"?

A: Beginning with the 2014-15 FAFSA, information is required of both legal parents if they both live with you, regardless of whether they are married. Information from both parents will be required on the FAFSA, regardless of the parents' gender or marital status, if:

1. Both parents are legal parents, defined as biological or adoptive parents; and
2. The student's legal parents live together.

Additionally, if your parents are a same-sex couple and were legally married in one of the14+ states (or the District of Columbia) permitting same-sex marriages, they are considered married for federal purposes and their information should be included in your FAFSA.

Q: Should I include my parents' e-mail address?

A: Refer to the "Help and Hints" box on the right side of the screen for clarification about e-mail addresses. Only enter an e-mail address if you want the federal processor to send your parent(s) an e-mail notification about your FAFSA application.

Q: How do I answer the question "How many people in your parents' household"?

A: Always include yourself (even if you don't live with your parents), your parent(s), both of them if married, or not married but living together, and brothers and sisters supported by your parents who cannot answer "yes" to any question in Chapter 2 (FAFSA dependency questions). Only include others if your parents will provide greater than 50% of their support.

Q: How do I determine the number of family household members attending college?

A: Always include yourself. And, of the people you included in your parents' household, enter the number of these household members attending college in the 2014-15 year. They must be taking at least two classes in a semester. Don't include parents.

Q: I have my parents' names, but not their social security numbers. Can I skip this?

A: No, if you are dependent, you must provide parent information, including their social security number(s). If your parents do not have a social security number enter "000-00-0000".

Visual Aid:

See that colorful blue bar on left indicating "PARENT"? We've begun to put in parents' information, right?

Parent Tax Information page
Frequently asked questions for this page:

Q: What is the IRS Data Retrieval Tool?

A: The IRS Data Retrieval tool allows students and/or parents to access their IRS tax return information needed to complete the FAFSA and transfers the data directly into the FAFSA from the IRS web site. This is the best way to provide tax return income information because it ensures that your FAFSA income answers are accurate.

Q: Why can't my parents use the IRS Data Retrieval Tool?

A: If your parents haven't filed their tax return electronically within the past two weeks or by paper through the mail within the past six weeks, tax information may not yet be available on the IRS database. Additionally, if your parents are married and filed separate tax returns, or are married but filed as head of household, or filed an amended tax return, or filed a Puerto Rican return, your parents are not eligible to use this tool. Also, if your parents owe federal tax and haven't paid it yet, their tax return will not be in the IRS database.

Q: Will this IRS Data Retrieval Process allow the IRS to look into my FAFSA and see my personal information or my parents' information?

A: No, the IRS cannot view your information or your parent(s) in this process. That would be in violation of federal privacy laws protecting you from invasion of privacy. The tool is only designed to populate your FAFSA from the IRS database automatically and quickly with your parents' tax return income answers.

Q: The message on this page is telling me I can't use the IRS Data Retrieval Tool for my parents' information. What do I do?

A: If you can't use the IRS Data Retrieval Tool or you decided not to use it, you must enter your parents' federal tax information, using a copy of their 2013 federal tax return as a reference. As you manually enter each item, click in the field and the "Help & Hints" box on the right of the screen will be updated to show exactly which line on the tax return to refer to for the answer. You can also refer to the questions further on in this chapter to find your tax answers.

Q: When I use the IRS Data Retrieval Tool, I'm seeing a warning message that I'm leaving the FAFSA web site. Did I do something wrong? Is this ok?

A: This is ok. All your FAFSA information is automatically saved and you're transferred to the IRS web site. Don't worry. When the IRS match is complete, you'll be brought right back to FAFSA online and returned to your application exactly where you left off.

Q: The transfer did not work. What do I do now?

A: Try this: Be sure to type in your parents' information in the IRS web site exactly as it appears on their tax return. Include a middle initial, if it's on their tax return. If it still does not work, cancel the transfer and you'll be brought back to your FAFSA. Grab your parents' tax return and start filling in the answers.

Q: Hey, some tax fields were not filled in by the IRS transfer, like my parents' wages field. Should I try the transfer again?

A: No, it's ok. Some items, such as wages, will not carry over from the IRS if your parents filed "married filing jointly". Get their 2013 W-2 forms and enter the information. Other items may be blank because they are blank on their tax return. This means the answer is "0" to these items. Put a "0" in those fields on this screen.

Q: I just completed the IRS transfer, but realized that I need to go back and make a correction to the transferred information. Is that ok?

A: No, do not make any changes to these items. Changing any income item included in the IRS transfer process will immediately place your FAFSA for selection for federal verification, requiring you and your parents (if dependent) to submit various income documents to the financial aid office. Your receipt of financial aid can be seriously delayed as a result. Really, DON'T DO THAT!!

Parent Financial Information page
Frequently asked questions for this page:

Q: My parents have not filed their income tax return yet, but will file a tax return soon. How do I answer these income questions now?

A: If you indicate that your parents *"will file a federal tax return"* you can estimate the answers with a previous year's tax return (2012), or your parents' 2013 W-2 forms or your parents' last pay stubs of the 2013 year. Don't worry…it is ok to estimate. You can correct your FAFSA later when their tax returns are completed.

Q: My parents have not filed their income tax return yet for 2013. Should I wait until they complete their tax return before I finish my FAFSA?

A: No, do not wait. It's ok to estimate their income answers. It's important to submit your FAFSA before your college financial aid deadline. You can correct this information later on.

Q: My parents are not married but live together. Should both parents complete the FAFSA with their information?

A: Yes, both legal parents (biological or adoptive) should file the FAFSA with both parents' information. This is a new change for the 2014-15 filing year.

Q: After I entered my parents' marital status, a message appeared stating that there is a difference between what I entered on the FAFSA and the filing status reported on my parents' federal tax return. What should I do?

A: This message is a warning that the FAFSA online edits detected a difference between your parents' reported filing status on their tax return and their marital status reported on your FAFSA. If their marital status is correct on your FAFSA, then just re-confirm it and move on. However, if you made an error, go back and put in their correct marital status.

Q: My uncle claims me on his federal tax return, but I live with my mother. Whose information should I put down in the parent section; my uncle's or my mom's?

> **A:** You should include only your mom's information on your FAFSA. The fact that your uncle claimed you on his tax return has no bearing on your FAFSA.

Q: My parents are a married same-sex couple, legally married in state permitting same-sex marriages. Should both parents' information be included in the FAFSA?

> **A:** Yes, both legal parents' information (biological or adoptive) should be included in the FAFSA. This is a new change for the 2014-15 filing year.

Q: My parents are not going to file a tax return for 2013. How do I complete the FAFSA?

> **A:** It's ok if your parents will not file a tax return. The web site will move you past any income tax questions automatically, if you indicate the status "will not file". Many families across the country live on nontaxable income or don't earn enough to be required to file a tax return.

Q: Where do I find adjusted gross income on my parents' tax return?

> **A:** You can find your parents' adjusted gross income on line 37 on Form 1040, line 21 on Form1040A or line 4 on the Form 1040 EZ.

Q: Where can I find the amount my parents earned from work?

A: Review the 2013 W-2 forms they received from their employer(s) to answer this question.

Q: Do I need to show my parents' unemployment benefits in the fields asking about my parents working?

A: No. Do not put any unemployment benefits in these fields. Unemployment benefits are already included in your parents' adjusted gross income on their federal tax return.

Q: What is a dislocated worker?

A: A dislocated worker is someone who has been laid off, will be laid off, or is receiving unemployment benefits. If your parent quit his/her job, they are not considered a dislocated worker. If you're not sure, it's ok to select "don't know".

Q: Will it hurt my chances for financial aid if my parents received benefits from these federal low income programs?

A: Just the opposite; your eligibility may increase if you or a family member received benefits in 2012 or 2013 from any of the following programs. Check each box that applies to you and your family.

☐ Supplemental Security Income (SSI)
☐ Food Stamps or Supplemental Nutrition Assistance Program (SNAP)
☐ Free or Reduced Price Lunch
☐ Temporary Assistance for Needy Families (TANF)
☐ Special Supplemental Nutrition Program for Women, Infants and Children (WIC)
☐ None of the Above

Q: A question on this page is asking me if my parents could have filed a 1040A or 1040EZ. What does that mean?

A: It could mean greater financial aid eligibility, if they qualify. If your parents filed a 1040 IRS tax form, and their income was less than $100,000 for the year, they did not itemize deductions, they did not receive alimony and they didn't own a business or farm, your parents qualify. Put your cursor in the answer box and look to the right of your screen in the Help & Hints box for more guidance. If you are still unsure, it's ok to select "I don't know".

Parent Financial Information Continued page
Frequently asked questions for this page:

Q: There is a question asking about the amount of income tax my parents paid. Should I include taxes paid to the state as well as federal taxes?

A: No. Do not include any state or local taxes your parents paid in 2013. This question refers to the amount of *federal taxes* paid and can only be found on their 2013 federal income tax return.

Q: Where do I find the amount of income tax my parents paid?

A: This figure is only found on their completed income tax return (not on their W-2 forms). On form 1040, look for this figure on line #55, on form 1040A, the answer is on line #35 and on the 1040EZ form, you will find the answer on line #10.

Q: Where do I find my parents' number of exemptions?

A: The word "exemptions" means the number of people including yourself that are dependent on your parents' income to live. On both forms 1040 and 1040A, look at line 6d. You will not find the number of exemptions on form 1040EZ. If your parents filed a form 1040EZ, leave this item blank.

Q: Some of these items don't apply to my parents. Can I leave them blank?

A: Yes, but only the ones that don't apply to your family. Check each box that applies to your parents. Skip any items that don't apply. When you check an item, a box will appear underneath that will allow you to enter the annual dollar amount received. If you are looking on your parents' tax return for an answer to an item in this section and it is blank on their return, skip it on this FAFSA screen. Check out the "Help & Hints" box on the right of the screen for additional guidance.

Q: Some of these items are already filled in, some with zeros and some are blank. How do I continue?

A: If your parents filed a tax return *and* successfully used the IRS Data Retrieval process, then some of the questions on this screen are automatically answered. Some items in this section are not found on a filed tax return. Look through the list of income items on this screen and check each one that applies to your parents. A box will appear under each of the checked items where you can enter the annual amount of income received in 2013.

Q: My parents didn't file a tax return. Do I need to complete this section?

A: Yes. Some of these items also apply to parents who didn't file a tax return too. Check each item that applies to your parents and fill in the 2013 income amount in the box that appears under each checked box.

Visual Aid:

Still see that colorful blue bar on the left side of this screen indicating "PARENT"? We're still putting in parents' information, right?

Q: What is "untaxed" income?

A: Untaxed income items shown in this section refer to money received by your parent(s) that is not taxed by the federal government. However, this form of income must be reported on the FAFSA.

Q: Some of these untaxed income items don't apply to my parents. Can I leave them blank?

A: Yes. Check any box that applies *only* if your parents received untaxed income from that source in 2013. Skip any item that doesn't apply to your parents. When you check an item, a box will appear underneath where you can enter the annual dollar amount received in 2013. If you are looking on your parents' tax return for an answer to an item in this section and it is blank on their return, the answer is "0" and you can skip that income item on this FAFSA page. Refer to the "Help & Hints" box on the right of the screen which provides additional guidance.

Some of the following untaxed income items may not appear on this screen if your parent(s) did not file a tax return or filed a 1040EZ. Don't be concerned.

- ☐ **Payments made to tax-deferred pension and savings plans;** Boxes A-D, codes D, E, F, G, H & S

- ☐ **IRA deductions to self-employed pension plan;** Line 28, and line 32 on Form 1040, or line 17 on the 1040A

- ☐ **Child support received** (not paid)

- ☐ **Tax exempt interest;** Line 8b on IRS Forms 1040 and 1040A

- ☐ **Untaxed portions of IRA distributions;** 1040, subtract line 15b from line 15a; 1040A, subtract line 11b from 11a

- ☐ **Untaxed portions of pensions** 1040 subtract line 16b from line16a; 1040A, subtract line 12b from line 12a

☐ **Housing, food and other living allowances paid to military, clergy and others**

☐ **Veteran's non-educational benefits.** Include disability, death pension and VA educational work-study allowances

☐ **Other untaxed income.** Include worker's compensation, disability and portions of health savings accounts from IRS 1040, line 25. **Don't Include**: student aid, earned income credit, additional child tax credit, welfare payments, untaxed social security or supplemental security income.

Q: How do I answer the question about parents' current balance of cash, checking and savings?

A: This answer refers to the total amount of money your parents have in their checking or savings bank accounts. Enter the dollar amount they have *as of the day you complete your FAFSA*. If the answer is "0", enter "0".

Q: What is meant by "net worth" in the question referring to investments and real estate?

A: "Net worth" means the value of the asset (investments, real estate, etc.) minus anything owed on it (mortgages, loans, etc.).

Q: How do I know what investments mean and what to include in this answer?

A: Check the "Help and Hints" box on the right side of your screen to see what investments to include. Many investments or assets should not be included in this answer, such as the house your parent(s) own, your family car, jewelry or their pension savings accounts.

Q: My parents own and operate a business. But, there's a message indicating some businesses shouldn't be listed. How do I know if I should report the value of my parents' business?

A: The net worth of a business should be reported only if it does not qualify as a family-owned and operated small business. Do not include the worth of a business or farm if your parents own and control more than 50% of the business and employ fewer than 100 full-time employees. Do not include a family farm that your parents live on and operate.

Take a break! Check the kids, bathroom run, check the score of the ballgame and head back to your computer....

Student Tax Information page
Frequently asked questions for this page:

Q: What is the IRS Data Retrieval Tool?

A: The IRS Data Retrieval tool allows students and/or parents to access their IRS tax return information needed to complete the FAFSA and transfers the data directly into the FAFSA from the IRS web site. This is the best way to provide tax return income information because it ensures that your FAFSA income answers are accurate.

Q: Why can't I use the IRS Data Retrieval Tool?

A: If you haven't filed your tax return electronically within the past two weeks or by paper through the mail within the past six weeks, tax information may not yet be available on the IRS database. Additionally, if you are married but you and your spouse filed separate returns, or you filed as head of household and you're married, or you filed an amended tax return, or filed a Puerto Rican return, you are not eligible to use this tool.

Lastly, if you filed your federal income tax return, but owe a tax payment you have not made yet, your tax return will not be available in the IRS database.

Q: Will the IRS Data Retrieval service allow the IRS to look into my FAFSA and see my personal information?

A: No, the IRS cannot view your information in this process. That would be in violation of federal privacy laws protecting you from invasion of privacy. The tool is only designed to populate your FAFSA fields from the IRS database automatically and quickly with your tax return income tax answers.

Q: The message on this screen is telling me I can't use the IRS data Retrieval Tool. What do I do?

A: If you can't use the IRS Data Retrieval Tool or you decided not to use it, you must enter your federal tax information, using a copy of your 2013 federal tax return as a reference. As you manually enter each item, click in the field and the "Help & Hints" box on the right of the screen will be updated to show exactly which line on the tax return to refer to for the answer. You can also refer to the questions further on in this chapter to find your tax answers.

Q: I'm seeing a warning message that I'm leaving the FAFSA web site. Did I do something wrong? Is this ok?

A: This is ok. All your FAFSA information is automatically saved and you're transferred to the IRS web site. Don't worry. When the IRS match is complete, you'll be brought right back to FAFSA online and returned to your FAFSA application exactly where you left it.

Q: I just completed the IRS transfer, but realized that I need to go back and make a correction to the transferred information. Is that ok?

A: No, do not make any changes to these items. Changing any income item included in the IRS transfer process will immediately place your FAFSA for selection for federal verification, requiring you and your parents (if dependent) to submit various income documents to the financial aid office. Your receipt of financial aid can be seriously delayed as a result. Really, DON'T DO THAT!!

Q: The IRS transfer did not work. What do I do now?

A: Try this: Be sure to type in your information in the IRS site *exactly* as it appears on your tax return. *Don't forget the spaces!* Include a middle initial if you have one on your tax return. If it still does not work, cancel the transfer and you'll be brought back to your FAFSA. Grab your tax return and start filling in the answers.

Q: Hey, some tax fields were not filled in by the IRS transfer, like the wages field. Should I try the transfer again?

A: No, it's ok. Some items will not carry over from the IRS, such as wages, if you filed "married filing jointly". Get your 2013 W-2 forms and enter the information. Other items may be blank because they are blank on your tax return. It's ok. This means the answer is "0" to these items. Put a "0" in those fields.

Student Financial Information page
Frequently asked questions for this page:

Q: I (and my spouse) have not filed my income tax return yet, but plan to file later on for 2013. How do I answer these income questions now?

A: If you indicate that you *"will file"* a federal tax return you can estimate the answers with a previous year's tax return (2012), or your 2013 W-2 forms or your last pay stub of the 2013 year. Don't worry…it is ok to estimate. You can correct your FAFSA later when the tax returns are completed.

Q: I (and my spouse) have not filed my (our) income tax return yet for 2013. Should I wait until I complete my tax return before I finish my FAFSA?

> **A:** No, do not wait. It's ok to estimate. You can use your 2012 tax return, your 2013 W-2 forms or pay stubs from 2013 to move through the FAFSA online process. You can correct your FAFSA later on when you complete your tax return. Remember that you must have your FAFSA submitted before college financial aid deadlines.

Q: After I entered my marital status, a message appeared reporting that there is a difference between my marital status reported on the FAFSA and the filing status reported on my federal tax return. What should I do?

> **A:** This message is a warning that the FAFSA online edits detected a difference between your filing status on your tax return and your marital status reported on your FAFSA. If your marital status is correct on your FAFSA, then just re-confirm it and move on. However, if you made an error, go back and put in your correct marital status.

Q: I'm not going to file a tax return for 2013. How do I complete the FAFSA?

> **A:** It's ok if you will not be filing a tax return. The web site will move you past any income tax questions automatically if you indicate the status *"not going to file"*. Many people across the country live on nontaxable income or don't earn enough to be required to file a tax return.

Q: Where do I find adjusted gross income on my tax return?

> **A:** You can find your adjusted gross income on line 37 on Form 1040, line 21 on Form1040A, or line 4 on the Form 1040 EZ.

Q: Do I need to show my unemployment benefits in the fields asking about my wages from working?

A: No. Do not put any unemployment benefits in these fields. Unemployment benefits are already included in your adjusted gross income on your federal tax return.

Q: Where can I find the amount I earned from work?

A: Look at your 2013 W-2 form that you received from your employer(s) to answer this question.

Q: What is a dislocated worker?

A: A dislocated worker is someone who has been laid off, will be laid off or is receiving unemployment benefits. If you quit your job, you're not considered a dislocated worker. If you're not sure, it's ok to select "don't know".

Q: Will it hurt my chances for financial aid if I received benefits from these federal low income programs?

A: Just the opposite; your eligibility may increase if you or a family member in your household received benefits in 2012 or 2013 from any of the following programs. Check any items that apply to you.

☐ Supplemental Security Income (SSI)
☐ Food Stamps or Supplemental Nutrition Assistance Program (SNAP)
☐ Free or Reduced Price Lunch
☐ Temporary Assistance for Needy Families (TANF)
☐ Special Supplemental Nutrition Program for Women, Infants and Children (WIC)
☐ None of the Above

Q: A question is asking me if I could have filed a 1040A or 1040EZ instead of the IRS form 1040 that I did file. What does that mean?

> **A:** Some tax filing services have their clients file the IRS form 1040 (also called the "long form") even if they only have wages and could have filed the easier and shorter 1040A or 1040EZ. If you could have filed a 1040A or 1040EZ, it could mean greater financial aid eligibility. The requirements are; you have filed an IRS form 1040 but your income was less than $100,000 for the 2013 tax year, with no itemized deductions, received no alimony and you don't own a business or farm. Put your cursor in the answer box and look to the right of this screen in the "Help & Hints" box for more guidance. If you are still unsure, it's ok to select "I don't know".

Student Financial Information Continued page
Frequently asked questions for this page:

Q: There is a question asking about the amount of income tax I paid. Should I include taxes paid to the state as well as federal taxes?

> **A:** No. Do not include any state or local taxes that you paid in 2013. This question refers to the amount of federal taxes paid and can only be found on your 2013 federal income tax return.

Q: Where do I find the amount of income tax I paid?

> **A:** This is not the amount of your tax withholding figure reported on your 2013 W-2 form. This figure is only found on your completed income tax return. On form 1040, look for this figure on line #55, on form 1040A, look for the amount on line #35 and on the 1040EZ, you will find the answer on line #10.

Q: Where do I find my number of exemptions?

> **A:** The word "exemptions" means the number of people including yourself that are dependent on your income to live. On both forms 1040 and 1040A look at line 6d. You will not

find the number of exemptions on form 1040EZ. IF this is the form you filed, leave this field blank.

Q: Some of these items don't apply to me. Can I leave them blank?

A: Check each box that applies to you. Skip any that don't apply. When you check an item, a box will appear underneath that will allow you to enter the dollar amount. If you are looking on your tax return for an answer to an item in this section and it is blank on your return, skip it on this FAFSA screen. Check out the "Help & Hints" box on the right of the screen for additional guidance or click the "**NEED HELP?**" link on the bottom of your screen.

Q: Some of these items are already filled in, some with zeros and some are blank. How do I continue?

A: If you filed a tax return and successfully used the IRS Data Retrieval process, then some of these questions on this screen are automatically answered. Some items in this section are not from a filed tax return. Look through the list of income items and check each one that applies to you. For each item you check, a box will appear underneath where you can enter the annual amount of income received in 2013.

Q: I didn't file a tax return. Do I need to complete this section?

A: Yes. Some of these items also apply to applicants who didn't file a tax return. Check any item that applies to you and fill in the 2013 yearly amount in the box that appears underneath.

Some of the following items may not appear on this screen if you did not file a tax return or filed a 1040EZ. Don't be concerned.

☐ **American Opportunity, Hope or Lifetime learning tax credits.** Line #49 on 1040 and line #31 on the 1040A

☐ **Child support paid**

☐ **Taxable earnings from Work Study, Fellowships or Assistantships**

☐ **Grant and scholarship aid reported to the IRS**. Look at your 1098T form from your college

☐ **Combat pay or special combat pay** Check this box if you have taxable amounts.

☐ **Cooperative education program earnings**

Visual Aid:

Still see that colorful blue bar on left indicating "STUDENT"? We're still putting in student information, right?

Q: What is "untaxed" income?

A: Untaxed income items shown in this section refer to money received by you that is not taxed by the federal government. However, this form of income must be reported on the FAFSA.

Q: Some of these items don't apply to me. Can I leave them blank?

A: Yes. Check any box that applies *only* if you received untaxed income from that source in 2013. Skip any item that doesn't apply to you. When you check an item, a box will appear underneath where you can enter the annual dollar amount received in 2013. If you are looking on your tax return for an answer to an item in this section and it is blank on your return, the answer is "0" and you can skip that income item on this FAFSA screen. Refer to the "Help & Hints" box on the right of the screen which provides additional guidance.

Some of the following untaxed income items may not appear on this screen if you did not file a tax return or you filed a 1040EZ. Don't be concerned.

☐ **Payments made to tax-deferred pension and savings plans;** Boxes A-D, codes D, E, F, G, H & S

- [ ] **IRA deductions to self-employed pension plan;** Line 28, and line 32 on Form 1040, or line 17 on the 1040A

- [ ] **Child support received** (not paid)

- [ ] **Tax exempt interest;** Line 8b on IRS Forms 1040 and 1040A

- [ ] **Untaxed portions of IRA distributions;** 1040, subtract line 15b from line 15a; 1040A, subtract line 11b from 11a

- [ ] **Untaxed portions of pensions;** 1040, subtract line 16b from line16a; 1040A, subtract line 12b from line 12a

- [ ] **Housing, food and other living allowances paid to military, clergy and others**

- [ ] **Veterans' non-educational benefits:** Include disability, death pension and VA educational work-study allowances

- [ ] **Other untaxed income;** Include worker's compensation, disability and portions of health savings accounts from IRS form 1040, line 25. Don't Include: student aid, earned income credit, additional child tax credit, welfare payments, untaxed social security or supplemental security income

- [ ] **Money received or paid on your behalf** Include money received to pay bills, etc not reported elsewhere

Q: How do I answer the question about my current balance of cash, checking and savings?

A: This answer refers to the total amount of money you have in your checking or savings bank accounts. Enter the dollar amount you have *as of the day you complete your FAFSA*. If the answer is "0", enter "0".

Q: What is meant by "net worth" when they're referring to investments and real estate?

A: "Net worth" means the value of the asset (investments, real estate, etc.) minus anything owed on it (mortgages, loans, etc).

Q: How do I know what investments mean and what to include in this answer?

A: Check the "Help and Hints" box on the right side of this screen to see which investments to include. Many investments and assets should not be included in this answer, such as the house you own, your family car, jewelry or your pension savings accounts.

Q: How do I know if I should report the value of my business?

A: The net worth of a business should be reported only if it does not qualify as a family-owned and operated small business. Do not include the worth of a business or farm if you own and control more than 50% of the business and employ fewer than 100 full-time employees. Do not include a family farm that you live on and operate.

Sign and Submit page
Frequently asked questions for this page:

Q: Should I answer "YES" to the question asking if I am a preparer?

A: No. This question is for those who are in a consulting business and charge a fee to prepare FAFSA applications for their clients.

Q: One of the options to sign my FAFSA is to submit the FAFSA without signatures. Is that ok?

A: NO! You don't want to submit this application without signatures so leave that choice alone. *Really, don't do that.* If you do, your completed FAFSA will come to the college in a "REJECT" status. The Student Aid Report (SAR) you receive from the Federal Processor as well as the college financial aid office will notify you that you must sign the application (at least one parent too, if you filed as dependent) before the college can offer you any financial aid.

Q: One of the options to sign my FAFSA is to submit the FAFSA with both my and my parent's signatures on a printed signature page. Is that ok?

A: You can submit your FAFSA with a printed signature page but this will delay the processing of your FAFSA. I strongly recommend that you (and one parent listed on your FAFSA, if you are a dependent filer) get a federal PIN to sign the FAFSA electronically. Doing so speeds up the processing of your FAFSA and gets it to your college(s) in approximately 4 to 5 days. A signature page will work but it will slow things down for weeks. Go to chapter 3 for guidance for obtaining a PIN or click on the link in this online screen and it will take you to the PIN web site. After you get your PIN, you'll be brought back to this page to continue.

You're almost there!

Read the student certification statement and click the "Agree" circle when you're done reading. If dependent, have your parent(s) read their certification statement and click "Agree" when they have finished reading it. Click on the "SUBMIT MY FAFSA NOW" button. There it is!! You've done it!

After you submit your FAFSA, your confirmation page will appear which tells you your FAFSA was transmitted successfully into the federal database for processing. It also provides general information about the colleges you've chosen and your eligibility for federal student aid, but don't take the financial aid amounts literally. The college financial aid office determines your final award for federal student aid based on your enrollment, and other factors. Print the page for your records or write down your confirmation number. If you provided a valid e-mail address, the federal processor will e-mail you your confirmation automatically.

You're done. Congratulations!

Make sure to close your browser before getting up and leaving. Now, if you're interested in what happens next, you can peek ahead to Chapter 6, called *After the FAFSA: Read Your Mail or E-mail,* to find out what happens after submission of your FAFSA.

Q: Now that I've submitted my FAFSA, should I send a copy of my tax return(s) to the Federal Processor?

A: NO! You do not want to mail any personal income documents, letters, thank-you cards, etc. to the Federal Processor. *Really, don't do that.* Actually, the computer company hired by the U.S. Department of Education to process your FAFSA gets thousands of pieces of mail from FAFSA applicants all over the country. That's why they have a very big and hungry shredder. It even eats staples….

* * *

Chapter. 5

The Alternative:
Filing The Paper FAFSA

*Note: Skip this chapter if you're filing
your FAFSA online.*

Can you file a FAFSA application by paper anymore?

A friend of mine received an electronic book reader for her birthday recently and she loves it. You can download complete books and magazines and read them just about anywhere. I'm noticing more and more people with these readers every day. Personally, I still like to carry a soft paperback in my back pocket to pull out whenever I have a few minutes to myself.

Yes, at least for the present, digital printing is active and producing printed books and magazines daily. And so, the paper financial aid application is available as well. Filing the paper FAFSA is not as popular with the general public as filing the FAFSA online, but the same results can be achieved no matter which way you file. In other words, filing the paper FAFSA will qualify you for the same kind of financial aid and you will be considered for the same amounts of financial aid as online filers. Time wise, filing the FAFSA on paper takes longer than online filing. Filing the FAFSA on paper requires you to pay closer attention to your college financial aid deadlines. The paper FAFSA is more difficult and time-consuming, but that's why you bought this book, right? I'll walk you through each step and each question.

Before we even talk about completing the paper FAFSA, we have to get our hands on one, which used to be a lot easier than it is today. Back in the 20th century (am I really this old?), the U.S. Department of Education mailed hundreds of thousands of paper FAFSA application booklets to every college and high school across the country each year. To get a paper FAFSA back then, you simply walked into any college financial aid office or high school guidance office and asked for a copy or two of the FAFSA.

Today, the paper FAFSA is not as easily available, but it can be had. We actually need the internet (ironic, isn't it?) or someone who can use the internet for us to print out a paper FAFSA. We can also use the phone as a last resort. Here are your choices:

- Go to the Federal online FAFSA application web site located at **www.fafsa.ed.gov** and select "FAFSA Filing Options". Select the 2014-15 School Year and print out a PDF version of the 2014-15 FAFSA. Or….
- Go to any financial aid office and ask them to print out a paper FAFSA for you (definitely my choice). Or….
- Call the Federal Student Aid Information Center at 1-800-433-3243 and order a copy of the 2014-15 FAFSA. It will be a week or so before it arrives in the mail, so take this into account in terms of how long this process will take. In other words, "chill" until the application is in your hands, but be mindful of you college's financial aid deadline.

After you have the paper FAFSA in hand and before we begin to put black-ink pen to paper (no pencil, ok?), we need to cover some basics as we ready ourselves to complete the FAFSA.

The Basics

Eligibility:

Are you eligible for financial aid? To be eligible for federal or state financial aid, grants, loans or work study, you must be a U.S. citizen or an eligible noncitizen (permanent resident). If you are neither of these, there are other immigration statuses as well as living in certain U.S. territories that can make you eligible for financial aid. Review the information on page 2 of the FAFSA booklet for more guidance. You also must be enrolled in an eligible academic program, not be in default on a previous student loan or owe grant funds previously received from the federal government, and you must demonstrate financial need.

Know your deadlines:

This is very important! Financial aid deadlines for filing the FAFSA vary from school to school. After you've decided which colleges you want to include on your FAFSA, call the college or log on to their college web site and find their financial aid application deadline. Write down the deadlines for each of these schools. Which one of these schools has the earliest deadline? You should file your paper FAFSA no later than *four weeks before that day* (the day of the earliest deadline). Submitting the FAFSA after a college's financial aid deadline could result in not being considered for some of their financial aid programs. Additionally, state financial aid programs carry their own application deadlines as well. Check the front page of the FAFSA booklet.

*As a side note, do not confuse college *admissions* deadlines with FAFSA *submission* deadlines. One has nothing to do with the other.

Get it together:

Before you begin, please check the following chart for important personal documents you should have on hand to ensure that you complete the application accurately.

DOCUMENT	Dependent Filer		Independent Filer	
	Student	Parent(s)	Student	Spouse
Social Security Card (Original or Copy) * You (the student) must have a valid social security number	✓	✓	✓	
State issued Drivers' License (if you have one)	✓		✓	
2013 Federal Income Tax Return (no state returns)	✓	✓	✓	✓
2013 Non-Taxable Income Information such as child support (not alimony), pension contributions, veteran's non-educational benefits such as disability, death pension, dependency compensation, etc. You can find this information on veterans benefit letters, court documents, etc.	✓	✓	✓	✓
2013 W-2 Forms (if any) received from employer(s)	✓	✓	✓	✓
Asset Information such as bank accounts, investments, real estate, business and farms.	✓	✓	✓	✓

"You", means YOU, the student: Parents, this is not your application, so when the FAFSA has the word "you" or "your" in any sentence or question, they are referring to "the student".

It's about time: You're going to need to commit some hours to this effort. Plan on it!

You must have a valid social security number to complete and file the FAFSA. Don't have one? Go get one at your friendly, neighborhood Social Security Office (SSA). For additional information (in English or Spanish), you can call the SSA at 1-800-772-1213 (1-800-325-0778) or go to its website at **www.ssa.gov** .

So now that you have the time and documents to complete the FAFSA, let's do it! Remember, it's ok to stop in the middle. If it's getting late and it's time to turn in, close up shop and re-open tomorrow. Just watch that college filing deadline, ok?

Do I need my parents' information to submit the FAFSA? Good question. To find the answer, take a brief walk through Chapter 2 and answer the 13 "yes" or "no" questions.

One last word:

There are no guarantees in life and no guarantees here either. Consider the art of fishing. You toss your line out, but you have no certainties that you'll pull in that trophy fish. You're applying for financial aid with no assurances you'll receive financial aid, grants, student loans or part-time jobs. How your college's financial aid office determines your eligibility for funding will depend on a number of factors, including the information you include on your FAFSA, when you submit the FAFSA (less money is available if you file after the deadline), the amount of financial aid funds the college has available, whether you are enrolled in an eligible academic program and other considerations. Keep in mind that depending on the college you want to attend and their cost of education, you may not qualify for any financial aid or only federal student loans.

As we begin, you'll notice that the sections in the paper FAFSA booklet are color-coded. All sections for students are colored in blue, and the parent sections are in purple. Keep this in mind to make sure you're entering the right information in the correct section. Use a black-ink pen to fill in the response circles and *fill in the space completely*. Do not use check marks or "x" marks.

Getting Started - Step One, (student), Questions 1 – 31. The application begins on Page 3 of the FAFSA Booklet → Turn to page 3 of the FAFSA.

This section requires some basic information about you, the student, including 31 questions that cross well into page 4 of the FAFSA booklet. Pull out your social security card and hold it close and let's start with Question #1. *Quick note: If any question in this step doesn't apply to you, you can leave it blank, except questions #8 & #23.*

Questions 1, 2, and 3: Enter your full name (**exactly as it appears on your social security card**). Place one letter in each block.

Question 4 to Question 7:

☆ Enter your house number and street name, including apartment # (if you have one) in question #4, leaving an empty block as a space between your house/building number and the name of your street. In Question #5, enter the city where you reside and the country you live in, if not the U.S. Enter the two letter code for your state in Question #6 and your zip code in question #7.

☆ If you think you might be moving in the future, put in your current mailing address anyway. If you move later on, file a change of address form with your post office. Your mail will follow you to your new address for a year. Oh, and let the college Registrar know your new address too. Hey, cover all the bases.

Question 8: Social Security Number

☆ Enter your (the student's) social security number, one number in each block space. Now check it against your social security card. *This is important!* This number *must* be entered accurately!

Question 9 through Question 12: Enter this basic information. If you don't have a driver's license, leave it blank.

Question 13: Your e-mail address

☆ Enter your e-mail address so the federal processor can e-mail a document called a Student Aid Report (SAR) to you. If you decide to use your e-mail address, use the one that you will be sure to check regularly.

Question 14: Are you a U.S. Citizen? Mark only one circle.

☆ Being a U.S. Citizen or eligible non-citizen is the same for financial aid purposes.

- Circle 1; Yes; I am a US citizen, skip question #15 and go to question #16.

- Circle 2; No, but I am an eligible noncitizen. Fill in question #15.

- Circle 3; No, I am not a US citizen or eligible non-citizen, fill in Circle 3 and move on to question #16.

☆ If you fill in Circle #3, refer to the helpful information about this status on page 2 of the FAFSA booklet.

Question 15: Alien Registration Number

☆ If you filled in Circle #2 above, enter your alien registration number from your alien registration card.

Question 16: Your marital status as of today, the date you sign your FAFSA

- Circle 1; Married or re-married
- Circle 2; Never married
- Circle 3; Divorced or separated
- Circle 4; Widowed

☆ If you consider yourself "separated", you can only indicate this status if your spouse (husband or wife) is not living with you in your residence.

Question 17: Month and year you were married, or remarried, or separated, divorced or widowed.

Question 18: The 2 letter state code of the state where you live

☆ Your state is where you file your state income taxes, or have a driver's license or vote or even have a library card. Do not put in the state where your college is located, unless, of course, you live in the same state.

Question 19: Did you become a legal resident of this state before January 1, 2009?

- Circle 1; Yes

- Circle 2; No

☆ If your answer is "Yes", skip question #20 and proceed to question #21.

Question 20: If you answered "No" in Question #19, indicate the 2 digit month and the four digit year you became a legal resident of your state.

☆ To qualify for state financial aid programs, you must be considered a legal resident in your state. Generally, you must be living in your state for a minimum of 12 months prior to the start of your college classes to be considered for state aid; however this may be different in your state.

Questions 21 & 22: Are you a male or female?

- Circle 1; Fill in if you are male, and go on to question #22.

☆ Most males between the ages of 18 through 26 must register with selective service. Please refer to the helpful information about this topic on Page 2 of the FAFSA booklet.

- Circle 2; Fill in if you are female, and skip question #22 and go on to question #23.

Question 22: If female, skip to question #23.

☆ The Selective Service System is a registration requirement for young men between 18 and 26 years of age. Selective Service registration was important when the U.S. Army had a draft in place. The draft ended a long time ago, but, registration is still a legal requirement in order to qualify for ANY federal money. Filling in Question #22 can automatically register you with the federal Selective Service system. For more information, or to register online, go to **http://www.sss.gov/** .

Question 23: Convictions for possession or sale of illegal drugs <u>WHILE</u> receiving financial aid

☆ Don't leave this question blank, *pu-lease*! This question asks if you (the student) have been convicted of an illegal drug offense while receiving federal financial aid.

- Circle 1; No. Answer "No" if you have never received federal student aid or if you never had a drug conviction while you were receiving federal student aid.

- Circle 2; Yes. If you must answer "Yes", you can still qualify for aid, but you should contact your financial aid office for help. You will be mailed a worksheet to determine if your conviction affects your eligibility. You may need to certify you went through a drug re-habilitation program as well. Continue completing the FAFSA.

Questions 24 and Question 25: The highest level of school completed by your father and mother

☆ Some states offer financial aid based on this information.

☆ Fill in the circle which indicates how far your parents went in their schooling.

Question 26: High School Completion Status

- Circle 1; Fill in if you achieved a high school diploma. Go to question #27.

- Circle 2; Fill in if you earned a General Education Development Certificate (GED). Skip question #27 and go on to question #28.

- Circle 3; Fill in if you were home schooled. Skip question #27 and go on to question #28.

- Circle 4; Fill in if none of these choices apply to you; go on to question #28.

☆ Read this question carefully. When you start taking college classes, will you have graduated high school? Do not answer the question as of today. The answer is based on your status *when you will start college.*

Question 27: High school information where you received or will receive your high school diploma

- Write in the name of your high school in the top box, the city where it's located in the lower box and the two letter code for the state.

Question 28: Will you have your first bachelor's degree by July 1, 2014?

☆ Read this question carefully. This doesn't ask if you *want* a bachelor's degree (BA). It is asking if you *have earned* one by July 1, 2014.

- Circle 1; Fill in "No" if you did not earn a bachelor's degree or will not have earned one prior to July 1, 2014.

- Circle 2; Fill in "Yes" if you will have earned a bachelor's degree.

☆ By the way, it doesn't matter whether you are using your degree or not. The question is not asking whether you're happy with your bachelor's degree, only if you have earned it. It also doesn't matter if the degree is domestic or if it was earned in a foreign country.

Question 29: When you begin the 2014-2015 school year, what will be your grade level in college?

- If you've never attended college, color in Circle #0.

- If you have attended college, but only earned a few undergraduate college credits, color in Circle #1.

☆ This question asks you what your college grade level will be when you start your college classes, not what you hope it'll be. Do not color in Circle #6 or #7 in this question unless you have completed a bachelor's degree program and you will be accepted for enrollment in a master's or professional degree (doctoral) program.

Question 30: When you begin the 2014-2015 school year, what degree or certificate will you be working on?

- Indicate the degree or certificate that you are working towards.

☆ This question asks what your goal is when you start your college classes. It is ok if you answer "Other/undecided".

Question 31: Are you interested in being considered for work-study?

☆ The federal Work-Study program provides part-time, on-campus and off-campus job opportunities. I recommend saying Yes, no matter what. It doesn't obligate you to a job and it keeps your options open.

> OK, good work! Take a break, bathroom run, check the kids, stretch and go grab some water or a soft drink. Catch the score of the game and let's get back to it after a few minutes.

Step Two (Student), Questions 32 – 45. Questions in this section are about income and assets for you (the student) if you are single, widowed or divorced. Or, if you are married or remarried as of the day you are completing the FAFSA, answer these questions including information regarding your husband or wife. Also, remember…no pennies. Round up or down to whole dollars.

Question 32: For 2013, have you (the student) filed your federal IRS income tax return as of today, the day you're completing this FAFSA?

- Circle 1; Fill in if you have already completed your tax return.

- Circle 2; Fill in if you haven't done your tax return yet, but you will.

- Circle 3; Fill in if you will not file a federal income tax return. Skip questions #33 to #37 and go right to question #39 on page 4 of the FAFSA booklet.

Question 33: What income tax return did you file or will file for 2013?

☆ To determine what federal form you filed, look at the top left corner of your federal tax return page.

- Circle 1; Fill in if you completed the IRS 1040 form.

- Circle 2; Fill in if you filed IRS 1040A or 1040 EZ forms.

- Circle 3; Fill in if you filed a foreign tax return. See page 2 for more information on this topic in the FAFSA booklet.

- Circle 4; Fill in if you filed a return in Puerto Rico or another U.S. territory. See page 2 for more information on this topic in the FAFSA booklet.

☆ If you filed a foreign tax return, use the numbers on the tax return, but convert them into U.S. dollars. Use the web site listed in the instructions on page 2 of the FAFSA booklet (www.federalreserve.gov). If you have a tax return from other territories, use the numbers from these tax forms.

Question 34: For 2013, what or will be your tax filing status?

- Circle 1; Fill in if you are filing as single.
- Circle 2; Fill in if you are filing as head of household.
- Circle 3; Fill in if you are filing a married joint return.
- Circle 4; Fill in if you are filing a married separate return.
- Circle 5; Fill in if you are a qualifying widow(er)
- Circle 6; Fill in if you don't know.

Question 35: If you filed, or will file a 1040, were you eligible to file a 1040A or 1040 EZ?

☆ How do you know? If you filed a form 1040, and your income was less than $100,000 for the year, you did not itemize deductions, receive alimony, or file schedule D (capital gains) and you don't own a business or farm, you can answer "Yes" to this question. If you're not sure, it's ok to indicate "Don't know".

Question 36: What was your (and your spouse's) adjusted gross income for 2013?

☆ From your tax return, look for the line that says "Adjusted Gross Income" which is line 37 on Form 1040, line 21 on Form1040A or line 4 on the Form 1040 EZ.

Question 37: Your (and your spouse's) income tax for 2013.

☆ This question asks how much tax you paid to the IRS. This is *not* the amount of your tax withholding shown on your 2013 W-2 form. This figure is *only* determined by completing your income tax return. On form 1040, look at line #55, on form 1040A, it's line #35 and on the 1040EZ, find the answer at line #10.

Question 38: Your (and your spouse's) exemptions for 2013.

☆ The word "exemptions" means the number of people, including yourself, who are dependent on your income to live. This number may be and can be zero, if someone else claimed you (such as your parents). On both Forms 1040 and 1040A you can find the answer on line 6d. Exemptions are not an item on the IRS form 1040EZ.

Question 39: How much did you earn from working in 2013?

☆ Regardless of whether you file a tax return or not, enter the amount of money you earned at any and all jobs in 2013. Look at your W-2 forms for 2013 for yourself and your spouse. Find the amount on line 7 + line 12 + line 18 of the form 1040 or line 7 of the 1040A or line 1 from the form1040EZ. Cash income you received but did not record on any tax returns, also counts for the FAFSA. If you are not sure of the amount, make a good estimate.

Question 40: How much did your spouse earn from working in 2013?

☆ Regardless of whether you or your spouse filed a tax return, or a joint tax return, enter how much your spouse earned at any and all jobs in 2013 (Put in a zero if you are single, separated or divorced). Look at his/her W-2 forms for 2013 for total wages. Remember, there may be more than one W-2 form. Cash income you received but not recorded on any tax returns, also counts for the FAFSA. If you are not sure of the amount, make a good estimate.

Question 41: As of today, what is your (and your spouse's) total current balance of cash, savings and checking accounts?

☆ Enter the total amount, rounding to whole dollars. Don't include student financial aid funds.

Question 42: As of today, what is the net worth of your (and your spouse's) investments, including real estate?

☆ "Net worth" means the value of the investment minus anything owed on it (mortgages, loans, etc.). The total figure entered here should *not* include the net worth of the home you live in.

Question 43: As of today, what is the net worth of your (and your spouse's) current business and/or investment farms?

☆ The net worth of a business should be reported only if it does not qualify as a family-owned and operated small business. Do not include the worth of a business or farm if you own and control more than 50% of the business and employ fewer than 100 full-time employees. Do not include a family farm that you live on and operate.

Question 44: A-F; Student's Additional Financial Information:

☆ Let's do this one question at a time.

A) Education credits.

- Enter the amount indicated on your tax return.

☆ On your federal tax return, look at line #49 on IRS form 1040 and line #31 on the form 1040A. If the line is blank, put in zero.

B) Child support you paid (not received) because of a divorce or separation agreement or as a result of a legal requirement.

- Enter the amount of child support you paid for the 2013 year. Don't include alimony.

C) Taxable earnings you received in 2013 as a result of participating in federal Work-Study or as part of an assistantship.

☆ Federal Work-Study is a federal financial aid program.

D) Taxable student grant and scholarships reported to the IRS in your 2013 adjusted gross income.

☆ This includes AmeriCore benefits, as well as grants and scholarship portions of college assistantships for master's or doctoral programs.

E) Combat pay or special combat pay.

☆ Only enter taxable amounts included in your adjusted gross income. Do not include untaxed pay found on your W-2, box 12, code Q.

F) Earnings from work under a cooperative education program offered by your college.

☆ Check this box if you received income earned from work from a cooperative education program at your college.

Question 45: Student's 2013 untaxed income; A-J

☆ Let's do this one question at a time.

☆ In most cases, untaxed income is money not reported on an income tax return, and, therefore, the government does not collect any portion of it. Report your total annual amount in whole dollars (no cents). Do not report weekly/monthly income figures. If a type of income doesn't apply to you, leave it blank.

A) Payments you made to tax-deferred (you pay taxes later in life) pension and savings plans.

☆ Usually you'll see this on your W-2 forms from your employer. It would be reported on the W-2 form in boxes 12A through 12D, involving codes D, E, F, G, H & S.

B) Pension deductions to IRA plans

☆ An IRA is a type of pension plan for self-employed people, such as a KEOGH) and other qualified plans. Look at your federal tax return, line 28, plus line 32 on Form 1040, or line 17 on the 1040A. This item is not on form 1040EZ.

C) Child support received (not paid) for any of your children.

☆ This is money you get from someone else for supporting your children. Don't include foster care or adoption payments.

D) Tax exempt interest income.

☆ Tax exempt interest can be found on line 8b on IRS Forms 1040 and 1040A.

> Parts E & F of this question can be confusing, but don't fret. Just have your tax return handy and follow my lead, do a little math with the right numbers from the right tax return lines.

E) Untaxed portions of IRA distributions (self-employed pensions).

☆ On IRS Form 1040, **subtract line 15b from line 15a** to determine the answer. On IRS form 1040A, **subtract line 11b from line 11a** for the answer. This item is not on form 1040EZ.

F) Untaxed portions of regular pensions.

☆ On IRS Form 1040 **subtract line 16B from line 16A**. On form 1040A, **subtract line 12b from line 12a**. This item is not on form 1040EZ.

G) Housing, food and other living allowances paid to you, if you are a member of the clergy or military.

☆ *Don't include* on-base military housing or the basic military housing allowance.

H) Veterans non-educational benefits.

☆ Include disability, death pension and VA educational work-study allowances. Look for your benefit letters from the VA.

I) Other untaxed income.

☆ Include things like worker's compensation, disability and untaxed portions of health savings accounts (line 25 on IRS form 1040) from your tax return. *Don't include* student financial aid, social security benefits, supplemental security income, Workforce Investment Act benefits, on-base military housing, combat pay, foreign income exclusion or flexible spending plans.

J) Money received or paid on your behalf not reported elsewhere.

✮ Include money that someone gave you to pay your bills, etc.

Break time!! Take a breather and come back in 10 to 15 minutes…you deserve it!

Step Three (student), Questions 46 – 58. Are you a dependent or independent FAFSA filer?

✮ Answer each question "Yes" or "No".

✮ The answers to the questions in this step will determine if you (the student) qualify to complete the FAFSA as an independent student (you do not need to provide parental information) or a dependent student (you must report parental information). There are 13 "Yes" or "No" questions. These questions are the same questions listed in Chapter 2 of this book.

✮ If you answer "Yes" to at least one question, then you are an independent FAFSA filer and you can skip the parent section, (Step 4), and go directly to Step 5 on page 8 of the FAFSA booklet. If you answer "No" to *every question* in this section, you are a dependent FAFSA filer and should go to Step 4 and complete it with your parent's information. Step 4 is on page 6 of the FAFSA booklet.

✮ There are certain special conditions that can qualify you as an independent filer, even if you answered "No" to every question. Special circumstances might qualify you to get financial aid without parent information, but you'll need to work with an advisor in your college financial aid office. See chapter 10 for more information.

Step Four (parent), Questions 59 – 94.

In this section, your parents' personal and income information will be requested,

> **QUESTION TIME: Who or what is a parent (for the purpose of completing the FAFSA)?**
>
> **For FAFSA purposes, a parent is a biological parent or an adoptive parent.** A step-parent is considered a "parent" for FAFSA purposes only if he/she is still married to the biological or adoptive parent, or he/she adopted you as well. If you live with grandparents, foster parents, older brothers or sisters, a legal guardian, friends' parents, uncles or aunts, these people are not parents, for this application.
>
> So, if you live with a guardian, legal or otherwise, and they didn't adopt you, you may be able to file your FAFSA as an independent filer, but this may fall under a special circumstance appeal. Stop here, put your pen down and call your college financial aid office for help.
>
> If your parents are divorced or separated, and living apart, you will include only one parent on the FAFSA, the one you've lived with for most of the year. If the other parent you're not living with claimed you on his/her federal tax return, it doesn't matter. Now, if the parent you're living with re-married and you now have a step-parent, you must include the step-parent's information too. Parent verbal or written agreements do not matter for financial aid purposes.
>
> If you're not living with your parents, you still need their information. Let's keep going.

Question 59: What is your parents' marital status as of today? Fill in one circle only.

- Circle 1; Never married

- Circle 2; Unmarried and both parents live together

- Circle 3; Married or re-married

- Circle 4; Divorced or separated

- Circle 5: Widowed

☆ For <u>all</u> except Circle #2 (single), go to question #60. For Circle #2, go to question #61.

Question 60: Month and year your parents were married, re-married, separated, divorced or widowed

- Indicate the month and year of your parent's current marital status

☆ Answer question #60 if you filled in Circles #1, #3 or #4 in question #59. If you filled in Circle #2, skip this question.

Questions 61 through 68:

- Enter the names (full last name and first initial), birthdates and social security numbers of your parent's here.

☆ <u>NEW for 2014-15</u>: The FAFSA will be referring to "parent 1" or "parent 2" as either your father/mother/step-parent. Information from both parents will be required on the FAFSA, regardless of parents' gender or marital status, if:

1. Both parents are legal parents, defined as biological or adoptive parents this also includes legally married same-sex couples; and

2. The student's legal parents live together.

You can decide which parents' information you will use to answer questions 61 – 64 or questions 65 – 68.

☆ Remember, if you are living with only one parent, report only that parent's information and leave the other circles empty.

If your parents don't have a social security number, enter 000-00-0000.

Question 69: Your parents' e-mail address

- Enter your parents' e-mail address here, if one is available; enter one letter or number in each box.

☆ Enter your parents' e-mail address if you want the federal processor to contact them to acknowledge that your FAFSA has been processed. If you do include an e-mail address, be sure it's one that they check regularly.

Question 70: What is your parents' state of legal residence?

- Write in the 2 letter state code of the state where your parents live (the one(s) you live with).

☆ Their state of legal residence is where they file their state income taxes, have driver's licenses or where they vote. Do not put in the state where your college is located, unless, of course, they live in the same state.

Question 71: Were your parents residents of their state before January 1, 2009?

- Circle 1; "Yes" Skip to question #73

- Circle 2; "No" Continue to the next question.

Question 72: If the answer in question #71 is "No", provide the month and year legal residency began for the parent who has lived in the state the longest.

☆ If you can't determine when your parents' "legal residency" began, enter the date they started living in their sate.

Question 73: How many people are in your parents' household?

- Write in the number of members of your parent's household.

☆ Include:

➔ Yourself (even if you don't live with your parents)

➔ Your parents (obviously)

➔ Your parents' other children only if your parents provide more than ½ of their support or they can answer "No" to all questions on the FAFSA Independent/Dependent Checklist

➔ Other people supported by your parents (More than ½ of their support) and they are supported between July 1, 2014 and June 30, 2015

☆ Remember, children or other people can qualify to be included here *only* if your parents pay significantly for their support. If they just live under the same roof as your parents, that doesn't count.

Question 74: How many people in your parents' household (from question #72) will attend college between July 1, 2014 and June 30, 2015?

- Indicate the total number of family household members (including you) that will be attending college during this time.

☆ Always count yourself as a college student. Do not include your parents. You may include other household members, only if they will attend during the 2014-2015 year and take at least two classes in a semester.

Question 75 through Question 79: In 2012 or 2013, did you or your parents or anyone in your parents' household receive benefits from these federal programs?

- Fill in the circle for each benefit program that applies to your parents' household.

Question 75: Supplemental Security Income (SSI)

Question 76: Food Stamps or Supplemental Nutrition Assistance Program (SNAP)

Question 77: Free or Reduced Price Lunch

Question 78: Temporary Assistance for Needy Families (TANF)

Question 79: Special Supplemental Nutrition Program for Women, Infants and Children (WIC)

Break time!! Take a breather and come back in 10 to 15 minutes...the parent income questions are next!

☆ If you don't have your parents' 2013 income documents (tax return, W-2 forms, unemployment paystubs, etc.), find them now! If your parents haven't done their tax return yet, you can estimate. That's ok. If estimating, get their 2013 W-2 forms, or last years' federal tax return (from 2012) or their last paystub(s) for the year 2013. Remember, NO state tax returns.

Parent Federal Tax Return Questions;

Question 80: For 2013, have your parents completed their IRS income tax return or another type of return listed in question #81?

☆ Choose only one circle to fill in:

Circle 1; Fill in if they have completed and filed their 2013 tax return with the IRS

Circle 2; Fill in if your parents will file a tax return, but haven't yet completed their tax return

Circle 3; Fill in if your parents will not file a tax return.

☆ If your parents will not file a tax return or do not have to file, (Circle #3), skip to *question #88*. No need to address other tax return questions.

Question 81: What federal income tax return did your parents file or will they file for 2013?

Circle 1: Fill in if it is IRS form 1040

Circle 2: Fill in if it is IRSA form 1040A or form 1040EZ

Circle 3: Fill in if it is a foreign tax return

Circle 4: Fill in if they file a Puerto Rican return or a return from another U.S. territory

☆ How can you determine what federal income tax return form is used by your parents? Look in the upper left corner of the tax return to determine what kind of return your parents are using.

Question 82: For 2013, what or will be your parents' tax filing status?

- Circle 1; Fill in if your parent is filing as single.

- Circle 2; Fill in if your parent is filing as head of household.

- Circle 3; Fill in if your parents are filing a married joint return.

- Circle 4; Fill in if your parents are filing a married separate return.

- Circle 5; Fill in if your parent is a qualifying widow(er)

- Circle 6; Fill in if you don't know.

Question 83: If your parents filed, or will file a 1040, were they eligible to file a 1040A or 1040 EZ?

☆ If your parents filed an IRS 1040 tax return, they may have had the option to file a 1040A or 1040 EZ federal tax return.

☆ How do you know? If they filed a form 1040, and their income was less than $100,000 for the year, they did not itemize deductions, received alimony, or filed schedule D (capital gains) and they don't own a business or farm, you can answer "Yes" to this question. If you're not sure, it's ok to answer "I don't know".

Question 84: As of today, is either parent whose information is included in your FAFSA a dislocated worker?

☆ A dislocated worker means one or both parents have been laid off, or will be laid off from their jobs or are receiving unemployment benefits. If your parent(s) quit their job(s), they do not qualify as a dislocated worker.

☆ Have your parents' tax return handy because you're going to look for specific line items for the next few questions (question #85 through question #89). If the answer to a question is zero or the question does not apply you, answer zero ("0"). *Don't leave any question in this section blank.*

Question 85: What was your parents' adjusted gross income (AGI) for 2013?

☆ AGI is located on IRS form 1040, line 37; line 21 in the 1040A and line 7 on the 1040EZ.

Question 86: What did/will your parents pay in income tax for 2013?

☆ Don't look to your parents' 2013 W-2 forms for this one. This amount is calculated on their tax return. Find line 55 (2nd page) on IRS form 1040 for income tax paid; line 35 on the 1040A or line 10 on the 1040EZ for income tax paid.

Question 87: Enter your parents' number of exemptions for 2013.

☆ Exemptions are on IRS form 1040 and form 1040A, line 6d. For the 1040EZ, enter "1" if single or "2" if married. Exemptions are not on form 1040EZ.

Question 88: How much did your parent 1 earn from working in 2013?

☆ The easiest place to find this information is to look at that parents' 2013 W-2 form.

Question 89: How much did your parent 2 earn from working in 2013?

☆ The easiest place to find this information is to look at your other parents' 2013 W-2 form.

Question 90: As of today, what is your parents' total current balance of cash, savings and checking?

☆ Be sure to round the number to the nearest whole dollar for this question.

Question 91: As of today, what is the net worth of your parents' investments, including real estate?

☆ "Net worth" means the value of the asset minus anything owed on it (mortgages, loans, etc). There are a number of assets you should not include. Refer to the guidance on page 2 of the FAFSA booklet to determine what assets to include in your answer.

Question 92: As of today, what is the net worth of your parents' current businesses and/or farms?

☆ Do not include the worth of a business or farm if your parents own more than 50% of the business with fewer than 100 full-time employees.

Question 93: A-F Additional Parent Financial Information:

☆ Let's do this one question at a time.

A) Education credits.

☆ On their federal tax return, look at line #49 on IRS form 1040 and line #31 on the form 1040A. If the line is blank, put in "0". This item is not included on form 1040EZ.

B) Child support your parent(s) paid (not received) because of a divorce or separation agreement or as a result of a legal requirement. Don't include alimony.

C) Taxable earnings your parent(s) received in 2013 as a result of participating in federal Work-Study or as part of an assistantship.

☆ Federal Work-Study is a federal financial aid program.

D) Taxable student grant and scholarships reported to the IRS in your parents' 2013 adjusted gross income.

☆ This includes AmeriCore benefits, as well as grants (scholarship portions of college assistantships, master's or doctoral programs).

E) Combat pay or special combat pay.

☆ Only enter taxable amounts included in the adjusted gross income. Do not include untaxed pay found on their W-2 form, box 12, code Q.

F) If your parent is also attending college, include earnings from work under a cooperative education program offered by your parent(s) college.

- Enter wages received (if any) from this program.

Question 94: A-I Untaxed Income, From 2013:

☆ Untaxed income, whether reported on a tax return or not, is money that the government does not tax and therefore, does not collect any portion of it.

☆ Report their total annual amount of nontaxable income in whole dollars (no cents). Do not report weekly/monthly income figures. If a type of income does not apply, leave the question blank

☆ Let's do this one question at a time.

A) Payments they made to tax-deferred (they pay taxes later in life) pension and savings plans.

☆ Usually, you'll see this on their 2013 W-2 forms from their employer. It would be reported in boxes 12A through 12D, involving codes D, E, F, G, H & S.

B) Pension deductions to IRA plans

☆ An IRA is a type of pension plan for self-employed people (such as a KEOGH and other qualified plans). Look at their federal tax return, line 28, and line 32 on Form 1040, or line 17 on the 1040A. This item is not on form 1040EZ.

C) Child support received (not paid) for any of your parents' children.

☆ This is money your parents get from someone else for supporting their children, including you. Don't include foster care or adoptive payments.

D) Tax exempt interest income.

☆ Tax exempt interest can be found on line 8b on IRS Forms 1040 and 1040A.

Parts E & F of this question can be confusing, but don't fret. Just have your parents' tax return handy and follow my lead, do a little math with the right numbers from the correct tax return lines.

E) Untaxed portions of IRA distributions (self-employed pensions).

☆ On IRS Form 1040, **subtract line 15b from line 15a** to determine the answer. On IRS form 1040A, **subtract line 11b from 11a** for the answer. This item is not on form 1040EZ.

F) Untaxed portions of regular pensions.

☆ On IRS Form 1040 **subtract line 16b from line16a**. On form 1040A, **subtract line 12b from line 12a**. This item is not on form 1040EZ.

G) Housing, food and other living allowances paid to your parent(s) if he/she is a member of the clergy or military.

☆ <u>Don't include</u> on-base military housing or the basic military housing allowance.

H) Veterans non-educational benefits.

☆ Include disability, death pension and VA educational work-study allowances. Look for their benefit letters from the VA.

I) Other untaxed income.

☆ Include things like worker's compensation, disability and the homebuyer's tax credit (line 67 on IRS form 1040) from their tax return.

☆ Again, untaxed income, whether reported on a tax return or not, is money that the government does not tax and therefore, does not collect any portion of it. However, some sources of untaxed money are not counted for financial aid purposes.

Don't Include:

- Student financial aid
- Social Security benefits
- Supplemental Security income
- Workforce Investment Act educational benefits
- On-base military housing
- Combat pay
- Foreign income exclusion
- Flexible spending plans.

Whew! We're done with the parents' questions. Great work! You deserve a break. Take one and we'll reconvene in a few minutes!

Step Five (Students)

☆ Complete this step *only* if you (the student) answered "Yes" to any dependent/independent questions in Step Three. If you answered "No", to all questions in Step Three, skip this section and go directly to Step Six and start with question 103.

Question 95: How many people are in your household?

- Enter the number of people in your household.

☆ Include:

➔ You (and your spouse) don't include boyfriends/girlfriends, apartment mates, etc.

➔ Your children, only if you provide more than ½ of their support and you will continue to do so through the upcoming academic year

➔ Other people who live with you who are supported by you (you provide more than ½ of their support) and will continue to be supported by you between July 1, 2014 and June 30, 2015

☆ Remember, children or other people qualify to be included here *only* if you pay more than half of their yearly support. If they just live under the same roof as you and support themselves, that doesn't count.

Question 96: How many people in your household (Question #95) will attend college between July 1, 2014 and June 30, 2015?

☆ Always include yourself as a college student and your spouse, if married. Do not include your parents. Include others only if they are in your household and they will attend at least half time.

Question 97 through Question 101: In 2012 or 2013, did you (and your spouse) or anyone in your household (from Question #93) receive benefits from any of these federal programs?

- Fill in the circle for <u>all</u> that apply:

Question 97: Supplemental Security Income (SSI)

Question 98: Food Stamps or Supplemental Nutrition Assistance Program (SNAP)

Question 99: Free or Reduced Price Lunch

Question 100: Temporary Assistance for Needy Families (TANF)

Question 101: Special Supplemental Nutrition Program for Women, Infants and Children (WIC)

Question 102: As of today, are you (or your spouse) a dislocated worker?

☆ A dislocated worker means one or both of you have been laid off, or will be laid off from your job(s) or are receiving unemployment benefits. If you (and/or your spouse) quit your job(s), you do not qualify. If you're not sure, it's ok to answer "I don't know".

Step Six (All Students): Indicate which college(s) you want to receive your FAFSA information.

Questions 103: A – H

- Enter the six-digit school code or write in the name and address of the college. Include the two-letter code for the state where the college is located.

☆ You can enter this information for up to four colleges. For state aid consideration, place your preferred college first.

In Housing Plans;

- Circle 1 if you will live on campus in the college dormitories

- Circle 2 if you will live with parents and commute to the campus

- Circle 3 if you will live in a house or apartment off the campus grounds.

Step Seven (Students & at least one parent for dependent filers) Read, sign and date.

Question 104: Date this form was completed

- Fill in the blocks with the month and day you completed this FAFSA. Indicate the year by filling in the Circle for 2014 or 2015.

Question 105: Student (sign the application)

- Sign the form (you, the student) in box 1. A parent (from Step Four) should sign in box 2, if you are a dependent filer.

☆ If you or your family paid a fee for someone to complete your FAFSA or to advise you on how to fill it out, that person must complete questions 106, 107 & 108.

This should be completed *only* if you paid someone to fill out this FAFSA for you. If someone in a financial aid office helped you, skip this question. Leave it blank if you completed this FAFSA yourself. Why give someone else the credit?

College Use Only

☆ This section in the lower right corner of this page should be left blank unless a member of a financial aid office is helping you file as an independent student through a special condition. In that case, your financial aid advisor will complete this question.

☆ Now that the FAFSA is complete, be sure to make copies of pages 3 through 8 of the FAFSA booklet for your records. Remove the FAFSA application from the booklet and fold it and slip it into an envelope. Address it as follows and include a return address. Please make sure you put the right amount of postage on the envelope. There are regular postal rate increases. It will be returned without the right postage.

Don't forget to mail it…..

Federal Student Aid Programs,
P.O. Box 4691
Mt. Vernon, IL 62864-0059

You're done!!!! Be sure to look for next year's edition of Fast Tracking the FAFSA, (2015-2016) to guide you through the 2015-16 FAFSA. We'll do this dance again next year!

By the way, if you are thinking of sending anything along in the envelope with your FAFSA, think again. The Federal Processor is only interested in your signed FAFSA. Anything else, like tax returns, personal letters, thank you cards, etc, goes directly to a shredder.

* * *

Chapter. 6

After the FAFSA:
Read Your Mail or E-mail

C ongratulations on completing your FAFSA!
You've completed the most important step in the financial aid process. It's a great feeling to know that you are in the game and ready to see the score. You'll soon receive mail or e-mail to let you know how well things are going and what additional steps you will need to take to keep the ball rolling.

The following is a description of what happens after you click that FAFSA online "submit" button, or you drop your paper FAFSA into the mailbox. When you're in the game, you need to know how the game plays out, right?

The most important bit of advice I can offer you right now is to make sure you read your mail or e-mail regularly and often. Yes, really!! Even though you've accomplished the challenging task of completing the FAFSA, the task at hand now is to communicate and respond, particularly to the ones who will determine and confirm the awards you're looking for; the college financial aid office, for one. But don't ignore other important messages from federal and state financial aid agencies too.

After receiving the results of your FAFSA, the financial aid office will be writing to you by regular mail, by email or even through texting to request additional information, or letting you know how much funding they've awarded you, or how to accept your awards. Set up a place or routine where you will read your mail regularly and respond in a timely way. Don't fool around here! Not responding to requests from the financial aid office can result in lost dollars!

Your FAFSA will be heading to a place called the Federal Processor; a computer company hired by the U.S. Department of Education to analyze your FAFSA and perform some matches with other federal databases, like the Social Security Administration (they check citizenship), the Department of Homeland Security and the Veterans Administration.

If you completed the FAFSA online and signed the FAFSA with your electronic federal PIN (see Chapter 3), your FAFSA will be processed and ready for you and your college to review in approximately four to six days. If you completed and mailed the paper FAFSA, or did your FAFSA online, but signed and mailed a paper signature page, your FAFSA will be processed within four to six weeks. Either way, when the Federal Processor has finished processing your FAFSA, you will receive a document called a Student Aid Report (SAR) by e-mail with a link to access your Student Aid Report (SAR) online.

The Student Aid Report (SAR)

The Student Aid Report (SAR) is a document sent to you by e-mail or postal service that will report your application results, the college(s) you've listed on your FAFSA and any specific messages or problems found in your FAFSA. In many cases, the SAR is just informational and can be used to review your FAFSA information for accuracy, particularly to check that the Federal Processor sent your FAFSA to the right college(s). Be aware that there are a number of colleges around the country with the same name. The FAFSA won't do you any good if it's sitting in the wrong college database, right? Check the last page of the SAR and look at the colleges listed. These are the schools that received your FAFSA information.

You can use the SAR to make corrections to your FAFSA if you discover any mistakes. For instance, if you estimated your income when you completed your FAFSA and you now have actual numbers from your completed federal income tax return, you can make corrections on the SAR, sign it and mail it to the address listed. You can also go to the FAFSA Online web site to make the corrections online. Chapter 7 provides step-by-step guidance for making corrections to your FAFSA online or by paper using the Student Aid Report.

The Expected Family Contribution (EFC)

At the same time you receive your Student Aid Report, your college(s) will receive your processed FAFSA electronically. This information is used to determine your eligibility for federal financial aid, and in some cases, state financial aid. It includes eligibility calculations and something called the Expected Family Contribution (EFC).

The financial aid office uses this number (EFC) as an index for determining your eligibility for financial aid programs. It's also a "jumping off point" for determining the federal and state programs for which you qualify. So don't over-react to this number. Do not assume that this number is what your family is expected to contribute towards your college expenses.

Generally speaking, the lower the EFC, the better your financial aid will be. This, however, is not a hard and fast rule. Other factors could work against you. For instance, if you filed your FAFSA late, or your FAFSA was processed, but rejected because you forgot to sign it, or you are attending a high-cost school and they have limited financial aid funds, then your low EFC will not necessarily result in the financial aid you might expect.

Colleges May Require Additional Information (Federal Verification)

Some colleges may require additional forms and/or applications for financial aid, such as their own institutional application (easy to complete) or a fee-based form produced and managed online by a private company which some private colleges require. To find out about these possible requirements, contact your college's financial aid office or check their web site.

Federal Verification: Colleges may contact you if they require additional information and/or documents to verify information on your FAFSA. This may happen if you've made an error, or if the Federal Processor selected your FAFSA for a process called **federal verification**. The college will inform you of this selection or you can check your Student Aid Report. Don't get nervous; this is not an audit the college is doing. This is just an error correction process. So, for example, if they review your tax return transcript from the IRS, and they compare the income on it to the income on your FAFSA and they find an error, they will simply correct it and that's it!

Here's what to do: Gather the requested documents (only what the financial aid office asks for). Complete a verification worksheet if required (some colleges don't use a worksheet). Make copies of the documents (never send originals) and send them with the worksheet to the financial aid office.

Important: If you used the IRS data release tool when you completed your FAFSA online or later to make corrections, your tax IRS information is considered verified and you do not need to send IRS income tax transcripts to the financial aid office. Using this tool has been known to prevent selection for verification altogether. Lastly, if you use the IRS Data Release Tool, don't change or correct *any* of the income items later on. *This* is important!

Remember; don't delay in responding to the financial aid office with the requested information because the college can't give you your awards until this process is complete. If you have questions or problems, call the college financial aid office for help. Your college can reduce or eliminate your financial aid awards if you take too much time responding to their requests. Since most of their financial aid is awarded on a first-come, first-served basis, be sure to respond to requests for additional information or financial documents, in a timely manner. Don't be a couch potato! Delays can affect the dollar amount of your awards or the choice of your awards.

After you know your college(s) received your FAFSA information (by checking your SAR, right?), it may be a good idea to contact the financial aid office to see if any additional information is needed.

Financial Aid Award Notification

You've now applied for admissions and have been accepted to enroll at the college of your choice. Once your college financial aid office reviews your FAFSA and any additional information you may have provided, they will determine your eligibility for financial aid and notify you electronically or by postal service. This communication, or award letter, is also called a financial aid award notification. This award letter includes information on your grouping of awards, or "financial aid package". It may include a mixture of grants, scholarships, work-study programs, college-sponsored funds, and/or loans.

> *Remember,* you will typically receive a financial aid award notice *only* from those colleges to which you have been offered admission.

Some colleges may require you to register for classes so that they can determine how much financial aid you'll need to cover your direct college expenses. This includes tuition, fees, room and board (if you live on campus). Check with the financial aid office at your college(s) of choice to find out when and how they award you.

Keep in mind that there are many different federal and state financial aid programs that you automatically applied for when you filed your FAFSA. If you add to this some college-based financial aid programs, you may find that your college award letter lists anywhere from one to a half dozen financial aid programs available to you to finance your education. The award letter will include specific information on each federal, state, or college program that has awarded you and the dollar amount awarded per semester or enrollment period from each program. Review the letter carefully for instructions on how to accept the award(s) and to see if you need to complete any additional paperwork. Keep in mind, however, that depending on the college you want to attend and their cost of education, your award letter may consist of federal student loans only.

One last thought about the financial aid award letter. Don't lose track of the acceptance deadlines set by some colleges. If you miss this deadline, you could lose the whole financial aid award package and you could be writing a *really* big check.

Compare Financial Aid to Your Bill

IMPORTANT: When you receive the bill from your college for semester charges, check your award letter and compare the money awarded to you against the charges in your billing statement. The financial aid may be listed on your bill as well. Do your awards cover the entire balance or is there a remaining amount that you are expected to pay out of your own pocket? Also, does your financial aid offer include any student or parent loans? Are the loan amounts reasonable to you? Remember, federal student loans must be repaid and the monthly payment could be steep.

It is also possible that the financial aid office awarded more financial aid than you need to meet your billed expenses. That's ok and beneficial; you can use this money to help with the cost of books and supplies, transportation and even living expenses.

I know How Much Financial Aid I'm Getting and It's Not Enough!

So, here you are. You've received your college financial aid award letter, you know how much money you're getting, and you know what the college is charging you. But, it's still not enough to make this college affordable. There can be any number of scenarios that contributed to this outcome.

- The college may have run out of financial aid funds from programs with limited funds before they received your FAFSA, or

- The college didn't have enough funding to help all the applicants, or

- The direct college costs are just too high (tuition, fees, room & board).

Whatever the reason, the reality is that there is a "gap" between what the college expects you to pay and what you can afford to pay. Is there a solution, or do you need to find a different college to attend?

Of course, finding a lower cost school is always an option and should be strongly considered if there's time and you've been accepted for enrollment at another college. If you decide to stay with your current school of choice, there are a few additional options you can consider.

- Check with the college to see if they offer interest-free payment plans that allow you to break up the amount you owe into 4 or 5 equal monthly semester payments. For example, if your remaining balance on your fall semester bill is $1000 and due in August, you may be able to use the college's interest-free plan to pay $200 a month for five months, beginning in August and ending in December.

- Consider living off-campus in a more reasonably priced room or apartment or simply commute from your parents' home. In many areas around the country, rooms or apartments may be the more reasonably-priced option compared to your college's dormitory rate.

- If you do decide to live on-campus, choose your meal plan carefully. You will have a number of options to choose from which may save you considerable money. See Chapter 9 for guidance.

- Contact the college financial aid office to ask if there is any chance of adjusting your award package. Sometimes, schools have some flexibility and can make adjustments, for example, if you've made an error on your application, or you've enrolled in additional classes or your living arrangements have changed. If you have special circumstances or your family's financial situation has worsened since completing the FAFSA, make sure your financial aid office is made aware of this. These special circumstances may help to increase your financial aid. If this is something that has happened to you, go to Chapter 10 for guidance.

- You and/or your parents can take out additional federal student loans to help meet college expenses that are not covered. Federal parent loans taken out by your parents on your behalf to cover any of your college costs will require a credit check. One of your parents will need good credit. The federal program is called Parent Loans for Undergraduate Students (PLUS).

* * *

Chapter. 7

After The FAFSA;
Oops, I Made a Mistake!

*W*hat? *After all we've been through together, you've found a mistake on your filed FAFSA?* Relax. No worries. It happens. If you filed the paper FAFSA, keep reading. If you filed your FAFSA online, move to the "Online FAFSA" section on the next page.

By the way, if you want to have the results of your FAFSA sent to an additional college, an easy option is to call the federal processor at 1.800.433.3243. You will need to provide your Data Release Number (DRN) in order for them to assist you. This number can be found on your Student Aid Report (SAR) in the upper right corner of the cover page or online in your account on FAFSA on the Web at **www.fafsa.gov**. You can find it on the "My FAFSA Page" after you log in. It's also provided in the upper right corner of your Confirmation page that you either printed out or was e-mailed to you after completing the FAFSA. You can also have your FAFSA results sent to an additional college(s) through your Student Aid Report or by going through the online FAFSA process.

Correcting the Paper FAFSA

If you've found anything you'd like to correct on your paper FAFSA, the following are the simple steps you should take to make corrections.

- Look at the Student Aid Report (SAR) that you received in the mail.

☆ It's a 10-page document you received from the Federal Processor that tells you whether your FAFSA was successfully processed and to which colleges your FAFSA was sent (See Chapter 6). If you misplaced yours, call the Federal Student Aid Hotline at 1.800.433.3243 and ask for another copy.

- In the Correction Section, find the field you want to correct and fill in the new information.

☆ There are a few pages listing the information you entered with an empty space provided to the right of each item. This is where you can enter a new corrected value. This is the "Correction Section" of the SAR.

You may add an additional college or two on your paper Student Aid Report, but you can only process a maximum of four colleges through the paper process.

> Remember, you can correct as many items as you wish at one time. Once you're done, sign it and have your parent sign it (dependents only) and mail it to the address listed on the SAR. Don't forget your return address on the envelope and enough postage to get it there.

Correcting the Online FAFSA

If you found any information in your online FAFSA that's incorrect, the following steps will guide you through the correction process. You can make as many changes as you wish at this time. Remember, if you make corrections in the student sections, you'll need to sign the correction with your (the student's) federal PIN. If you are changing information in the parent sections, you'll need your PIN as well as your parent's PIN to sign the corrected FAFSA.

Screen Navigation Tip:

Go to the FAFSA online web site located at **www.fafsa.ed.gov** . Under the term "Returning User?" (by the green "Login" button), click the first menu item "Make a correction". You'll be brought to the Login Page.

- At the Login page, put in your name (full & correct name as it appears on your social security card), social security number and your date of birth. Click on the "Next" button.

- You'll be brought to the My FAFSA page which will show your application status, (such as your FAFSA was processed successfully), the dates you submitted your application and when it was processed. In the lower half of the page, you will see a choice under the heading *"You Can Also"* titled "Make FAFSA Corrections". Click on this link".

- The following page asks you to enter your federal PIN number and to create a new password. Click the "NEXT" button. If a red box with an error message appears, you may have entered your PIN incorrectly; try entering it again. If the same error message appears, click the link "I forgot/Don't know my PIN to retrieve your actual PIN number. Once you have your PIN, retrace your steps back to this point.

- You've now reached the "Correction Introduction page" where you can select the top menu item, "Making corrections to a processed FAFSA" to learn more about making corrections online. Click the "NEXT" button to continue.

- You should see your actual submitted FAFSA application, beginning with the Student Demographic page with all your information displayed exactly as you entered it. Select the tab at the top of the screen that indicates the section where the item you wish to correct is located. You can also scroll down to the bottom of your screen and click on the "NEXT" button until you've reached the page where the exact item of information you want to change is displayed. You may have to click through a few screens to get there.

- Enter the corrected value into the field(s) you want to correct.

- Scroll down to the bottom of the screen and click on the "SAVE" button. Once you have made all your corrections, click the "Sign and Submit" tab at the top of this screen until you're brought to the "List of Changes" summary page. This page shows you which sections you've made corrections to as well as the specific items to which you've made corrections. Check your corrections here. If you're satisfied, click the "NEXT" button. You'll be brought to the "Sign and Submit" page.

- Does the Sign and Submit page look familiar? It should. It's the same page you encountered when you first completed your FAFSA and were ready to submit it. On this screen, enter your federal PIN number to sign your correction. If information was corrected in the parent section, your parent needs to sign electronically with his/her PIN as well.

- Click on the "Agree" button for the terms and conditions. Then, click the "Submit my FAFSA now" button.

☆ Your final page is the Confirmation page. It shows that you've successfully completed and submitted your FAFSA corrections. This screen also contains the confirmation number of this transaction as well as the Data Release Number you can use later if you want to add a college to your FAFSA. If you provided a valid e-mail address, a copy of this screen was e-mailed to you. Or, you can print this screen for your records by clicking the "Print this Page" button on the bottom of your screen.

The correction will be processed and changed on your FAFSA in the federal database. Your corrected FAFSA will be transmitted to all the colleges to which you originally sent your FAFSA. You're done!

Common Mistakes

The following is guidance for the most common application errors and how to fix them.

Missing signature: You may have forgotten to sign your paper FAFSA or chose the online option to submit your FAFSA without signatures.

Another possible scenario is that you signed the FAFSA but forgot to have your parent (if dependent only) sign it or get a PIN and sign it.

- Paper FAFSA: Use the paper SAR to sign the signature page and mail it in. Include your parent's signature if you are a dependent filer.

- Online FAFSA: Follow the online steps previously outlined. After logging in, you'll be brought to the "My FAFSA page" where you'll clearly see the message that your application is on hold due to missing signatures. The next page will ask you if you want to sign your application using a federal PIN or print a signature page which you can sign and mail. I suggest using a federal PIN, since it is by far your fastest option. If you do, enter your PIN on the "Sign with a PIN page" and click "Agree" to the terms. Submit your FAFSA. Print out your confirmation page for your records by clicking the 'Print" button on the bottom of the screen.

Incorrect income items: It's easy to make mistakes on the FAFSA, especially when you have to think about tax paid, taxable and nontaxable income, etc….it's enough to make your head split!

- Paper FAFSA: Use the paper SAR correction pages and, referring to your tax returns or other income documents, make the corrections. Make sure to sign the signature page too and mail the corrections section to the address listed.

- Online FAFSA: Follow the online steps previously outlined and navigate to the student or parent income section. When you've finished making your correction(s), click the "Sign and Submit" tab at the top of your screen to reach the Sign and Submit page Enter your PIN to sign it. Don't forget your parent's PIN if you are correcting parent information.

I changed my name:

- First, you should change your name at the Social Security Administration (SSA). When that change has been processed, you can apply for a new Federal Student Aid PIN using your new name. To apply for a new PIN, go to the PIN Web site at **www. pin.ed.gov** and click "**Apply for a PIN**".

- You should also change your name on your FAFSA. Use the SAR for a paper correction or go to FAFSA on the Web to make the change online.

I used the wrong social security number:

- If you filed a FAFSA using an incorrect social security number (SSN), you can change that SSN by either entering the correct one on the paper Student Aid Report (SAR), or by asking the financial aid office at one of the colleges listed on your SAR to change it for you. Otherwise, you must file a new FAFSA with the correct SSN.

Incorrect marital status:

- Your marital status should not be changed unless your answers were incorrect on the day your FAFSA was submitted. So, if you got married or divorced after the FAFSA went out, *don't* change it.

- If you did answer this question incorrectly, make the correction on the paper SAR. Sign the signature page and mail it to the address provided.

- If working online, follow the steps previously outlined and navigate to the Student Demographic page to change your marital status or the Parent Demographic page if you need to change your parent's marital status. When you're done, move to the Sign and Submit page and submit it after signing the correction with your PIN. Don't forget your parent's PIN if you are correcting parent information.

Adding a college:

- You may add a college or two using the paper process through your Student Aid Report (SAR). Enter the name and address of your additional college(s) and if possible, the college's six-digit federal school code. Sign the SAR in the signature section and mail it to the address indicated. Be sure to provide sufficient postage and your return address.

- For the online process, at the Login page, put in your name (full & correct name as it appears on your social security card), social security number and your date of birth. Click on the "NEXT" button.

- You'll be brought to the "My FAFSA page" which will show your application status, such as your FAFSA was processed successfully as well as the dates you submitted your application and when it was processed. In the lower half of the screen, you will see a menu of choices under the heading *"You Can Also"*. Click on the link entitled "Make FAFSA corrections".

- The following screen asks you to enter your federal PIN number and to create a new password. Click the "NEXT" button. If you get a red box with an error message, you may have entered your PIN incorrectly; try entering it again. If the same error message occurs, click the link "I forgot/Don't know my PIN" to retrieve your actual PIN number. Once you have your PIN, retrace your steps back to this point.

- You've now reached the "Correction Introduction page" where you can select the top menu item, "Making corrections to a processed FAFSA" to learn more about making corrections online. Click the "NEXT" button to continue.

- You should see your actual submitted FAFSA application, beginning with the Student Demographic page with all your information displayed exactly as you entered it. Select the School Selection Section tab from the top of the screen. You will be brought to the "School Selection Summary page" which will show the schools you already selected.

- Click the "Add a School" button to reach the "School Selection page". Here, on the left of your screen, you can search on the name and address of the college or enter the six-digit school code on the right side of the screen and hit the "SEARCH" button.

- When the college you'd like to add appears in the "Search Results" box, click in the small box to the left of the school name and click the "ADD" button in the center of your screen. Once you see that your newly added college is listed on the right of your screen in the "Selected Schools" box, you may click the "NEXT" button. Select your housing plans for this college and then save your changes by clicking the "SAVE" button. Click the "Sign and Submit" tab at the top of your screen and you're brought to the "List of Changes" correction summary page. Scroll down to review the changes you've made. You can print this page by clicking the "Print this Page" button (make sure you're connected to a printer). If you're comfortable with your corrections, click the "Submit" button.

* * *

Chapter. 8

Don't Believe The Naysayers: Common Misconceptions About Financial Aid

Government financial aid programs, grants, loans and work-study jobs have been around for a long time (since the 1960's). So naturally, there are a lot of people out there who think they know the score and want to share their opinions on the subject with you. How can you tell if they are correct? I've attempted to address at least some of these misconceptions below in the hope that I can give you a good sense of what financing for college is really about.

- *I have to live in a box under a bridge to qualify for financial aid.*

While it certainly can't hurt to be financially strapped, many working families can qualify for financial aid. In fact, most students who are U.S. citizens or permanent residents of any income level can qualify for at least a federal student loan, if they meet other basic eligibility requirements.

- *There's an income cutoff for eligibility in the financial aid system.*

Income, both taxable and non-taxable, is important, but the determination of whether you qualify for grants (free money) is not just based on your income. Other factors are considered as well, such as the size of your family, the number of people in your family attending college, and your choice of college. I've encountered families with incomes over $100,000 who are eligible for grants, and I've also counseled families with incomes averaging $50,000 who do not qualify for grant funding. Don't pay any attention to this slice of misinformation. Even high income FAFSA filers who don't qualify for grant funds can qualify for federal student loans, as long as they meet the basic eligibility requirements.

- *I won't qualify for financial aid if my family owns a house, or has money in the bank.*

Here's some really good news about assets. Some assets are not considered when determining financial aid eligibility and your family's house is one of them. Other assets that don't count are your car, jewelry, your brother or sister's money, cell phones, computers, or any kind of pension or retirement savings accounts that are yours or your parents'/guardians'. So complete the FAFSA. You may be very pleasantly surprised.

- *A student needs good grades and high SAT scores to receive financial aid.*

Many colleges have institutional programs, such as merit scholarships, which they offer to high academic achievers. However, of the $185 billion or so in federal government financial aid, the lion's share of this money is based only on financial need and not on grades at all.

- *College is too expensive for my family.*

That's just not true. There are literally thousands of colleges around the country that are reasonably priced and the quality of their educational programs is worth the investment. The federal government offers over $185 billion in financial aid. Many states and colleges kick in their funds too, which in the end, could result in an education at little or no cost to you. With that said, please remember that depending on the college you want to attend and their cost of education, you may only qualify for federal student loans.

- *We have a lot of personal debt, so we should be eligible for more financial aid.*

While there is a lot of good news about applying for financial aid, this topic is not one of them. Personal debt such as credit cards or car loans isn't considered in the federal financial aid formula that determines financial aid eligibility. If, however, you've used credit cards to handle required living expenses, contact the financial aid office to inquire if that information can be useful.

- *I must own a computer and have internet access to apply for and receive financial aid.*

This is simply not true. While it may be more convenient to apply on your home computer, there is a wealth of places where public access to computers and the internet is within easy reach. Also, the paper FAFSA is still alive and well. You can reference Chapter 5 in this book to apply for financial aid on paper.

- *I have to be admitted to a college before I apply for financial aid.*

Not true. You do not have to be admitted to any college or university to apply for financial aid. You have to be admitted to a college to **receive** the financial aid you qualify for!

- *If I apply for financial aid, will it hurt my chances of being admitted to my college?*

Most college admission offices practice "need-blind" admissions, which mean the applicant's need for financial aid has no effect on the admissions decision. There is no penalty for applying for financial aid.

* * *

Chapter. 9

How To Pay for College: Money-Saving Tips

How to pay for college is a broader discussion than choosing the most affordable school. Naturally, deciding on an affordable college is a major step towards dealing with the impending storm of expenses, but it's not the only step. Filing the FAFSA and applying for scholarships is all about finding money, or resources to pay for college. But if you don't pay close attention to your annual college expenses, you're missing the whole picture.

There are financial choices to be made <u>after</u> you settle on a college... choices about tuition, meals and other expenses that can mean the difference in thousands of dollars lost or saved.

In this chapter, I'll review what college costs are and how financial aid pays for them. I'll go over public versus private college choices as you consider your financial options. I'll also review the different ways you can manage your money while in college to keep your costs down. You'll want the financial aid you've been given to closely match your college expenses.

What are College Costs?

College costs or expenses keep rising; and at first glance, many college and university price tags appear to be beyond the reach of most families. The list price or "sticker" price is the total of what's referred to as *direct educational expenses*. Direct educational expenses include tuition and fees, room and board (if you are living on campus), books and supplies. Net price (the actual amount a student pays) is the list price or "sticker" price of direct expenses minus your awarded financial aid. Essentially, financial aid is applied as a discount to the list price of the college.

- Tuition and Fees is what the college charges for the classes you're enrolled in. Usually, the college will set a price per credit hour. On the average, one class is generally three credits or 3 x the cost per credit hour. Colleges can charge by the credit hour or charge a flat rate for a group of classes, such as one flat charge for taking four or more classes. In this case, your cost is the same whether you take four, five or six classes.

- Room & Board refers to charges you'll deal with for living in college residence halls and eating in the college cafeteria every day which is referred to as a meal plan.

- Books and supplies are an important and real college expense. In college, *you* are responsible for buying your textbooks. They are not given to you and you need to be prepared for this expense.

The Lower Cost of Attending a Community College:

Community colleges are often referred to as two-year colleges. They offer a number of degree options such as a two-year degree, referred to as an associate's degree, or one-year certificate programs offering classes that teach you marketable job skills. Classes taken in a community college can be transferred to any four-year college. Most credits will be applied toward achieving a bachelor's degree.

The cost of a community college is a more affordable option for many families. The sticker price is lower; therefore your financial aid goes further. The classes you take are comparable to those of a public or private four year college and you can transfer most, if not all of your classes to a four-year school (as long as you get a passing grade of "C" or better and the classes pertain to your degree program). Just think of the money you've saved when you transfer one to two year's worth of college credits from a lower-cost community college to a higher-priced, four-year college.

Many high school students don't view community colleges highly because they believe it's "just like high school". But that's simply not true. Community colleges offer substantial academic programs and vibrant campus life that can rival many four year schools.

Remember, the sticker price of any college is lowered when financial aid, including loans, is applied.

Financial Aid and College Costs; How does it work?

So, how does financial aid figure into the grand scheme of affording college? Financial aid, simply stated, is a *discount*. What the college's sticker price is doesn't really matter. What matters is how much of that sticker price you will be paying for *after* financial aid is applied. For example, let's say you're thinking about buying a car but its list price is out of your reach at $5,000. The salesman comes over and informs you that there's a 50% off sale today, so this car is actually being offered at a discounted price of $2,500. Of course, you jump at the opportunity because you realize that you can now afford the car at this discounted price. The sale price, or discounted price, is what you pay, not the list price....get it?

Financial aid can come in the form of grants, scholarships, loans or even part-time jobs. These funds primarily come from the federal government, but there are also college-based awards and funding available through many state programs. Money from all these different financial aid programs is managed through a college's financial aid office. The financial aid office is responsible for getting this money into your hands.

State Financial Aid Programs:

Most, but not all, states in the United States have their own financial aid programs for their residents living in that state. Usually you, and in some cases your parents, need to have lived in your state for at least 12 months to qualify, but this requirement may vary from state to state. There can be plenty of financial aid available from the state you live in, but there are catches. Some states will only let you use their award money if you attend college in-state. However, if you are living in a state that allows you to use its funding in an out-of-state school, don't be surprised if the amount of the award is reduced.

While a handful of states have their own financial aid applications, most states only require that you file the FAFSA to apply for their programs. Check out the web site of the college of your choice to find out more about state financial aid programs and how you can qualify.

Public vs. Private Colleges:

What about public versus private colleges? Tuition and fees are more expensive at a private college or university, because they don't receive state funding like public colleges do.

Private colleges may have higher tuition rates, but they usually offer higher amounts of financial aid. Their funding, which may include additional scholarships and grants, makes them more competitive with the lower tuition costs of public colleges. The downside to this abundance of financial aid is that there may be substantial loan money in their financial aid offer. Keep in mind that you will need to decide on how much loan debt you are willing to take on. It could get steep. However, using loans as a tool to help pay for your education is a good investment if you borrow wisely. By the way, if you are attending a private college in the state where you reside, it is possible to receive state financial aid there too.

Public colleges lower their tuition rates for state residents based on public funding they receive through the state. Out-of-state students will pay a higher tuition rate because the college doesn't receive state funding for non-resident students. For example, if you live in New Jersey (stop laughing…) and you decide to attend a public college in Delaware, you'll pay the more expensive out-of-state tuition rate at the Delaware public college because you are not a resident. If you are a resident of Delaware and attend Delaware public colleges, your tuition will be lower because the college is receiving public funding for you as a resident of the state.

Public colleges provide offers of college-based scholarships and grants to help discount their sticker price as well. If you attend a state college, you'll see lower tuition costs, but again, *only* if you are a resident of that state. Remember, you can qualify for state financial aid in addition to the money you qualify for under the federal financial aid programs.

How to Pay for College....After Choosing your College:

Maybe you've just been accepted to a college and decided to enroll there, or perhaps you're staring at your first college semester bill. Here are some tips I can offer that will hopefully make your college education less financially challenging. You have choices you can make and actions you can take to move towards this goal. Let's take a look at each;

- **Flat-rate tuition:** Many public and some private colleges charge their full-time students one flat rate for tuition, instead of a per-credit charge. For example, a student taking four classes (12 credits) is charged the same amount of tuition and fees as a student taking six classes (18 credits). Think about this for a minute; the average time a student is taking today to complete a four year degree is four and a half to five years. That's five years of tuition and fees, instead of four. That's a lot of extra money to shell out. If a student takes 15 or 18 credits a semester (five or six classes), and completes the degree in four years, he/she has just saved a full year of tuition and fees - a bundle of money! If this interests you, check your college to see if they charge flat-rate tuition.

- By the way, enrolling in summer classes can be tough if you're on a tight budget. Summer classes are almost always a per-credit charge and there is considerably *less* financial aid available in the summer to help you pay for them. Also, after the first day of class, many colleges won't allow you to withdraw from the class without some tuition charge.

- **Books and supplies:** Books and supplies are a big ticket item at colleges these days and a definite "price shock" when you're in the college bookstore. Some science and engineering textbooks can be as high as $300 each. *Yes, you heard me right!* Students, particularly those coming out of high school, are surprised that they have to buy these textbooks and just about everyone is appalled at the cost. I would estimate that you need to have about $140 for books and supplies for each class you plan to take, wherever you attend. Yikes! That's a lot of money just to buy a book! But, there are a number of ways to cut the cost of textbooks.

- **Libraries** – Most college libraries keep copies of the most popular textbooks on reserve. The downside is that you can't check them out so you have to do your reading in the library. Go often and early, usually there are not enough copies to go around.

- **Professor copies** – Some teachers keep extra copies of their textbooks in their office. You can ask the professor if you may borrow a copy.

- **Used books** – Many professors use the same textbook every semester. Students can sell their used books back to the college bookstore and in turn the bookstore makes them available for re-sale at a steeply discounted price. Please note that not all texts are available used.

- **Buy online** – Not only can you check for used textbooks online, but there are many web sites where you can buy the exact book you need for a discounted price. You'll need the book's international standard book number (ISBN). All colleges are required to provide you with the textbook name and ISBN number so you can be sure you are purchasing the exact textbook that will be used in your class.

- **Rent books** – This may be the smartest way to go. Rent your text books through the college bookstore or online. The cost of renting is considerably lower than buying, and once you're done with the book and the course, return the book and forget about it. If you rent online, you'll need the book's international standard book number (ISBN). All colleges are required to provide you with the textbook name and ISBN number so you can be sure you are purchasing the exact textbook that will be used in your class.

- **Becoming an RA:** Are you thinking of living in the college's residence halls (dormitories)? You know, it could cost anywhere from $10,000 to $12,000 each year for a bed in a room on campus and a meal plan. So, do you know what an RA is? It stands for Resident Assistant and it's not a financial aid program, it's a job!

  In fact, it's a part-time job working in the residence halls. You don't receive a paycheck, but a free room instead. That's equivalent to a $5,000 to $6,000 grant. Interested? The one downside is that you need previous experience living in the residence halls on campus to qualify, so you won't qualify for this position and its benefits in your freshman year. But after your freshman year, contact the Residence Life office at your college and find out when the hiring process starts and how to apply.

  During your freshman year, try to get a part-time job or volunteer in the Residence Life office or another office on campus. A recommendation from a director in a campus office can give you a leg up when you do apply for the RA position.

- **Choosing the right meal plan:** Many colleges require a student who lives in their on-campus dormitory (also called residence hall) to sign up for a meal plan. You have some options here that can end up saving you hundreds of dollars by using a little common sense.

  Many colleges offer a two-meal-a-day plan or a three-meal-a-day plan. When I first went to college, my mom was concerned I wouldn't eat. I was skinny as a rail so she signed me up for the maximum meal plan they offered at the time; 3 meals a day, every day. The truth is that I never ate breakfast growing up. Even today, I don't eat breakfast. I run out the door after only a cup of coffee. All those breakfasts I blew off during that first year was sheer profit for the catering company and the college.

  It seems silly, but not really. Parents, think about your child and their eating habits; and students, know how you eat and when. For example, if you are planning on leaving campus every Friday afternoon and returning Sunday nights after dinner each and every weekend of the academic year, you may benefit from taking the 5 day meal plan instead of the 7 day meal plan.

- **Check your college semester bill for the health insurance fee:** Laws in many states mandate that all colleges and universities charge their students a fee for health insurance. So, colleges include a charge on students' bills, (excluding some part-time student bills). The charge can be as little as $50.00 or as high as $1800.00 for the academic year, depending on the state your college is in. If you have health insurance of your own or you are on someone else's health insurance policy, have this fee cancelled and taken off your bill. Contact the student accounts or bursar's office at your college and find out how to deal with this charge.

- **Don't use credit cards. A pizza can cost you $47!** That's a regular size pizza with pepperoni and mushrooms costing about $11 which a student bought for himself and a few others while they were studying for finals. But with interest charges of 11% to 29%, compounded forever (it seems), that pizza ended up costing $47. Students and credit cards don't mix. Using plastic makes splurging easy and hard to keep track of. It is unnecessary debt. In fact, Congress recently put into place a new law in 2011 requiring a parent's consent for people under 21 years old to get a credit card. Parents, if you want to give your child some plastic for emergencies or to allow for some reasonable spending, consider a debit card which provides some limits and safeguards.

- **Take regular campus classes. Online classes carry extra fees:** It sounds great….doesn't it? Take a class at home and complete your school work online in your bathrobe at 12 midnight. Quite frankly, it is a wonderful option if you have difficulty making it to campus because of other responsibilities, geography, child care, etc. But if you can make it to campus, do so, because online classes carry extra college fees, usually called technology fees that the college uses to develop, finance and maintain an online network of class offerings. The fees can be an extra $100 to $500 or more per semester.

- **Watch the schools refund policy:** If you're thinking of dropping a class you are enrolled in, drop the course at the 100% refund level. All colleges and universities have what is called a *tuition refund policy* that allows students to cancel their enrollment in any class and not be charged the full cost of the class if they drop it early in the term.

- Colleges will allow students to drop a class up to and including the first day of class attendance and receive a full 100% refund of tuition and fees. Some schools extend this 100% refund period through the entire first week of the semester. But if it's only just one day after the 100% refund period, withdrawing from that class can cost you anywhere from 25% to 30% of the tuition and fees charge. If you wait another week, you could be facing a 50% charge. If you wait until the end of the fourth week of the term or anytime beyond that, you could be responsible for paying the full charge for the class. So make sure you are aware of your college's refund policy and drop your unwanted or unnecessary class during the 100% refund period.

Federal Work-Study Jobs: This is a financial aid program that provides for part- time opportunities on-campus as well as off-campus. But, there's more to this than a paycheck.

I have a story for you:

Let's say you and I work for a fast food restaurant and we both earned $6,000 last year. I earned my entire $6,000 at the restaurant, but you only earned $3,000 there. You had a second job and earned $3,000 in a federal work-study job on campus. When we file our income tax returns, we'll pay the same amount of tax. But when we apply for financial aid through the FAFSA for next year, you'll be more eligible for financial aid because your FAFSA will show an income of $3,000 and my FAFSA will show my full restaurant earnings of $6,000. That's because earnings from work study can't be included as income on the FAFSA application; and therefore, cannot be counted against you… it's a financial aid program. So while we have the same amount of money jingling in our pockets from our earnings, you will be eligible for more financial aid money than me next year.

Money you earn from work study goes into your pocket in the form of a bi-weekly check or direct deposit. National research shows conclusively that students working part-time hours on campus have better grades and graduate in higher numbers than non-work study students. And, if you ask most college administrators, they'll tell you that many of their colleagues began their careers as work-study students. Real jobs equal real job experience. Contact your financial aid office about qualifying for a work-study award.

College Financial Aid Ploys

This is one subject where you want to keep your money in your pocket.

There are numerous student loan games you'll see in the mail or online. Most often, they are mailed directly to student's and parent's homes, requiring money up front (usually in the form of "processing" fees) before paying out loan money.

- First, remember that federal student loans are determined through the FAFSA and only college financial aid offices will contact you about loan eligibility.

- **There's no up-front processing fee or credit check for a federal student loan**. There is a small federal fee, called an origination fee, <u>AFTER</u> you receive the funds through your college. Also, legitimate lenders offering private educational loans will not ask for an up-front fee either.

- If you get loan offers in the mail, review them with your financial aid counselor at your college. They can work with you if you want or need a loan and can help you to determine the best path for you.

- Be careful when looking for scholarships too. There are a number of ploys to part you from your money. You'll see a fair number of offers that claim they can find you private scholarship money....for a fee. Don't believe it. There are numerous free scholarship search engines on the internet that are fast, automatic, and can connect you with legitimate organizations offering money. Your guidance counselor or any financial aid office can connect you with easy and free scholarship search help. A list of free scholarship search engines is available on our web site; www.fafsafriend.com.

- Also, any scholarship that requires you to pay money up front should be viewed suspiciously. Legitimate organizations or agencies offering scholarships will never require you to pay a fee before the process is complete. Hang up the phone, close your browser or trash the letter.

* * *

Chapter. 10

Financial Hardships Or Special Circumstances: Qualifying For More Financial Aid

This chapter is written for you, if you or your family is experiencing a financial hardship or special life circumstances that have a negative effect on your finances and your ability to pay for college. Do not despair. You may qualify for more financial aid and here's why.

It doesn't matter whether this change occurred before or after filing the FAFSA. The FAFSA only considers last year's income information (your last full taxable year). If your financial circumstances have changed significantly for the worse, how do you tell the FAFSA? What is the most effective way to let them know? Read on and find out...it's easier than you think.

The financial aid office was given legal authority by Congress to recognize individual situations on a case-by-case basis and provide greater financial aid as a result. The legislators realized that you can't fit all family situations into a neat ribbon-tied box and, consequently, there is no way the FAFSA can account for everyone's individual family circumstances.

There is a *real good chance* that your college financial aid office can help you explain and document your unusual or difficult situation so that your financial aid can be **increased significantly.**

Please note: If you are a graduate student pursuing a master's or doctoral degree, your eligibility for federal or state financial aid programs is limited to student loans.

Because the FAFSA is based on last year's income, it doesn't ask for any information regarding your current financial situation as of today. This would make it seem that the financial aid world doesn't care.....*but it does.* Addressing this matter is a two-step process.

- Complete your FAFSA and submit it.

- Make your financial aid office aware of your current hardship or special life circumstances. Contact the financial aid office of each college you're interested in and ask for their advice. Colleges often have their own forms and procedures for addressing these situations. Each college may respond differently too. Be prepared for that. You'll be asked to write a letter explaining the details and providing an estimate of your income for 2014.

Here's what you should do for the second step. Contact your financial aid office and follow their procedures to address your special circumstances.

Some special circumstances that the financial aid office can work with you are:

- Divorce or separation (legal or otherwise) involving you or your parents.

- Death of a parent or spouse

- Loss or reduction in parent income caused by unemployment, under-employment or disablement.

- Unexpected medical or dental expenses that were incurred during the year.

- A natural disaster affecting your life or causing you or your parents to incur additional expenses you did not anticipate.

- Reduction in child support, alimony or income from a fixed income source, like social security, veteran's benefits, pension payout, etc.

- Negative conditions in the home resulting in separation from the home or loss of income and/or assets.

A financial aid counselor will explain how the process works at their college (it varies from school to school). They might be able to provide a quick estimate for you once you've provided the information and details they need to make a decision. By the way, don't wait for an engraved invitation. As soon as you've experienced an event that negatively affects your financial situation, contact the financial aid office.

Write your letter explaining the special circumstance(s). The letter does not have to be a literary masterpiece, ok? Just explain your situation in your own words. Type it on a word processor and spell-check it. If your situation involves more than one special condition, write about all of them. Describe the financial impact it has had on your life and that of your family's.

Here's an example of a letter you could write:

Date

Director of Financial Aid
Your College
Financial Aid Office
123 Main Street
My Town, My State

RE: Student ID#

Dear Director of Financial Aid:

I am requesting a review of my son Junior's 2014-2015 financial aid eligibility based on the fact that my husband and I are in the process of divorcing.

My husband and I have been separated and living apart since February 1, 2014. My husband moved out and is living in a separate place in His Town, His State. I am working with an attorney and can provide documentation if you need it. My income as reported on the FAFSA for 2014-2015 will be drastically reduced. Based on the current economy, my anticipated income will be approximately $22,000 for the 2014 year.

The reason for my loss of income is my husband is not providing any monetary assistance towards the household expenses.

I am submitting this appeal to you to consider these special circumstances in determining my son's financial aid awards. He is a good student and an active member of the student body.

Thank you for your time and consideration.

Sincerely,
Anyname Smith

The following are some of the special circumstances that a financial aid office may be able to help you with. I've included some helpful tips for writing your descriptive letter.

- **Loss of Job**: Describe how this event has impacted your finances. Include the separation date from the job and if or when you think you'll find another job. Provide realistic numbers as well as you can and whenever possible. For instance, if you lost your job don't say "*I'm making less money this year*". Rather, say it this way "*I estimate that I will make approximately $___ this year, down from $___ last year*". It's ok to estimate; that's what this process is all about. Also, include all other income like estimated unemployment benefits (don't include your children's income, if any). Document the loss of the job with a pay stub from a state unemployment office or a separation letter from your employer.

- **Separation or Divorce**: Many states don't have a status of "legal separation", but don't be concerned. The point to make here is that a parent or spouse physically left the house you live in and now lives elsewhere and that person no longer contributes to the family income. If he/she is still living in the family home, the marriage is still intact, and your request for more financial aid won't be considered. Indicate the precise date the separation happened and how much yearly income he/she took with them. It won't matter if you filed a joint income tax return. Trust me here. Many times, this is difficult to document, especially if spouses are not talking, so if this is the case, your cover letter might be enough. A copy of a lawyer's letter would be useful too. But if you can talk with the dearly departed, get a copy of a utility bill or cancelled check proving he/she is living elsewhere.

- **Death or Disability**: In this case, indicate the annual loss of income and estimate what your likely income will be for this year (2014). Provide the precise date of the death or disability, the expenses you've incurred (if any), and when you paid them plus any regular or additional expenses you'll be paying for in the future. In the case of a disability, indicate the possible length of time the person could be disabled. "*I estimate that my wife will be* *disabled from February 9th to November 1st"*. Document this situation with a letter from a physician. In the case of a death, include a copy of a death certificate.

- **Negative Home Conditions**: Try to describe the exact conditions as best as you can. It helps to shed light on your situation if you describe what occurred, and include dates, even if these adverse conditions have been ongoing for years. *"My Mom dropped me off at my uncle's house when I was 16 years old in June 2009. I haven't seen my mom regularly except for an occasional birthday visit". "I haven't seen or heard from her since May, 2011"*. If at all possible, include a letter from a high school guidance counselor on school stationary. It is a convincing piece of supporting documentation that many financial aid offices consider highly. If this is not a possibility, other documents you may want to include could be court or police records, or letters from a doctor, social worker, family or friends.

- **Unexpected Medical or Dental Expenses**: Document in writing the exact financial details of what occurred as well as describing the nature of the medical emergency and when it happened. Be sure to include detailed out-of-pocket expenses; not the expenses covered by insurance. Mention insurance premiums *only* if you need additional coverage as a result of this medical condition. Mention all future expenses, especially if they are for maintenance of health and quality of life. For example; *"I had to build a handicapped ramp and handicapped entrance ways to my house to accommodate wheelchair access" or "I have to pay $___ a month for home nurse care"*.

- **Reduction in Other Types of Income**: Give the exact financial details of what happened. Indicate what income was lost or reduced, such as child support, alimony, welfare, social security, etc. Provide the date the income changed. Indicate if you think you'll have this income reinstated and when that might happen. Provide as close to real numbers as possible. For instance, don't say *"I'm getting less child support this year"*. Rather, say it this way; *"I estimate that I will receive child support in the amount of $____ this year"*.

- **Natural Disaster:** Provide details of the event, including dates, description of what happened and how it affected you personally. Describe your loss of finances, including wages and/or business, property and related medical bills. If there was loss of life, include the circumstances and the financial impact this loss had on you and your family. Estimate as best as you can your loss of income and assets in dollars as well as your anticipation of future losses through the entire 2014 year. For example; *The following is a summary of expenses and losses in 2013 as a result of the El Reno tornado.*

  Temporary shelter - $2000.00, Medical expenses - $1500.00 (not covered by insurance), New car payments - $3600.00 annually (family car totaled), Loss of income - $15000.00 due to business closing, Funeral Expenses - $10000.00.

  I estimate that during 2014 my total income will be $_____, which is significantly less than my income in 2013.

After submitting your written explanation and any supporting documentation to the financial aid office, give it a little time. If you do not hear from them, follow up with a phone call to see if they have made a decision. You may be pleasantly surprised. Good luck!

Important: The types of financial aid awarded and the amount of money you may receive depends on what your difficult hardship is and the extent to which it has harmed you. For example, you lost your job but were able to find a new one. As a result, your total loss of income compared to last year is only a few hundred dollars. Chances are that this will not be considered significant enough to warrant additional financial aid.

Keep in mind, however, that depending on the college you want to attend and their cost of education, you may only qualify for federal student loans. Be prepared for that.

* * *

Chapter. 11

Losing My Financial Aid;
It Could Happen!

C ongratulations! You've successfully navigated through the process of completing the FAFSA and are in the running to qualify for funding set aside for you to help pay your college costs. But the funds you're being considered for come from federal and state programs that have rules. We've already covered the rules that govern how you apply and get financial aid. Now, we'll cover rules you must follow to *keep* your financial aid so you can use it for the purpose it was given; to pay your college costs. The fact is that there are things to be aware of and rules you need to follow to keep your money where it belongs.....in your hands.

I have a true story for you......

One morning, late in the fall semester, I received a phone call from a distraught and angry mother. It seems that she opened an envelope addressed to her daughter containing a revised college bill for the fall semester. The revised bill was a result of a change in her daughter's financial aid. In fact, her daughter's financial aid was completely missing from the billing statement. The bill indicated that thousands of dollars were due from the student and her family. The mom was understandably upset and had a number of choice words for me. When she calmed down, I told her that I couldn't share the specific of her daughter's financial aid without her daughter present (due to the federal privacy law), so I suggested that she and her daughter come to see me.

Sure enough, the following morning there were two upset and concerned visitors waiting for me in the financial aid office. I asked the student if I had her permission to talk about her financial aid with her mother present and she agreed. I started the conversation by asking the student one question; *"Why haven't you been attending any of your classes?"* The student averted her eyes and looked down toward the floor. Her mom was visibly stunned, looking first at me, then toward her daughter. *"Is this true"*? her mom asked. But, the student remained silent. I needed to explain what at first glance, appeared obvious; the federal government requires students to be attending their classes to remain eligible to receive financial aid. Since we couldn't confirm her daughter's attendance in any one of her classes, we had to cancel her financial aid for the semester.

The background to this story is that the student was driven to campus by Mom three mornings a week and dropped off at the library. She kissed her Mom goodbye and promptly walked to the student center, where she hung out with her friends until mid-afternoon and then walked back to the library to be picked up by her mom, never attending a single class.

It was a sad meeting and a sad day for all of us. Why she didn't attend her classes is anyone's guess. But, the moral here for parents is to keep the daily lines of communication open. How was your day? What classes did you attend today? …and so on. Students, if you're having problems, seek guidance. You need to take time to talk to someone about your concerns sooner rather than later.

Remember, if at any time it becomes clear to the financial aid office that a student has never participated in class during a semester or dropped out of class before the end of the semester, the financial aid office is required by law to adjust or cancel the financial aid for that semester. The student will then be obligated to pay out-of-pocket for the cost of these classes because their financial aid has been reduced or cancelled.

There are other situations to be aware of that can lead to the same result; lost dollars. The following are some of the major issues that may cause a student to lose financial aid.

- **Financial Aid Deadlines:** Ignoring college financial aid deadlines is the most common reason students lose out on financial aid, but did you know that states have financial aid application deadlines as well? Many states across the country provide their residents with significant funding opportunities to help cover the cost of college education, but if you miss their deadlines even by a single day, you could lose a hefty sum of money. If you are considering attending a college in the state where you reside, contact the college financial aid office and find out what the state financial aid deadline is and file your FAFSA in time to meet it.

- **Enrolling in Ineligible Courses/Programs:** This is basic. Not all courses or academic programs qualify for financial aid. Any class you enroll in must be for credit towards an eligible degree or certificate program. *Make sure you ask your college if the academic program of your choice is financial-aid eligible.* If you audit a class (meaning if you take the class without getting credit), you cannot receive financial aid to pay for it. Also, some classes simply don't qualify for financial aid and may be classified as continuing education.

  Information about programs and classes that qualify for financial aid must be posted on the college's web site or in their admissions materials, as required by federal consumer protection laws. Be sure to find out *before* you enroll.

- **Not Reading Your Mail or E-mail:** This sounds like a silly reason to lose financial aid. *Consider this*: You've moved to another house or apartment and didn't file a change-of-address form with your post office. Filing this form allows your mail to follow you to your new address for a full year. Instead, your mail continues to be delivered to your old address and the new person living there throws it out. Or perhaps you can relate to this scenario. Your mail is delivered to your home and someone in your household drops it in a desk draw without you ever seeing it. Why is this a big deal?

Here's the deal. For a high percentage of FAFSA applicants, college financial aid offices will request additional information or supporting documents to fix obvious errors or check your FAFSA. Often, and usually repeatedly, financial aid offices mail letters or e-mail notices asking students to supply additional financial documents; for example, federal tax transcripts or information on non-taxed income. If the student hasn't checked his/her mail or e-mail, then obviously he/she is unaware that the college is waiting for this information. Because of the student's lack of response to their repeated requests, the college finally cancels the student's financial aid awards.

Ok, you say, maybe I'm not so great at checking my mail, but I do get to it occasionally. Eventually, I will respond with the information the financial aid office wants. So I'll get my financial aid, right? Well…maybe. You see, some financial aid programs have limited money. This is why I am advising you to get your FAFSA submitted before the college financial aid deadline, so you can qualify when most of the financial aid funding is available. This money is usually awarded on a first-come, first-served basis. Other student's applications are being reviewed and awarded, while you're being passed by because you have not responded. By the time you get around to responding some or all of that good money may be gone; spent; history! And, once this limited money is gone, it's "wait until next year".

By the way, some schools require that you let them know within a certain period of time if you want the financial aid package that they've offered. If you don't respond to the instructions provided with your award letter, they will cancel your awards and give them to someone else.

Don't be a dummy. Find a place for your mail and *read it* regularly…e-mail too. Not all mail you receive will be asking you to do something. Some are just informational notices that you may find useful. If you don't understand what's in the letter, ask. Contact the financial aid office and they'll be happy to work with you.

- **Withdrawing Early from a Class or Classes:** Every college or university has its own semester or term tuition refund policy that will charge you a different percentage of tuition if you withdraw from a class early.

Let's say you drop/withdraw from a class early, for example, the third week of the semester. As a result, the financial aid office must review your eligibility for your financial aid and may need to reduce or outright cancel some of your funding. So, where once you had a bill that was completely paid for by financial aid, you are now left with a significant out-of-pocket balance, perhaps hundreds of dollars.

Don't withdraw from any class without discussing your best course of action with your academic advisor as well as your financial aid counselor at your school. Get the information you need to make a good decision.

- **Unofficially Withdrawing from School Before the Term is Over:** Have I said this before? The federal government requires students to be attending their classes to remain eligible to receive financial aid. If you decide to leave school, and float off into the night without letting anyone in the school know you've left, the financial aid office won't be able to confirm your last date of attendance. As a result, your financial aid will be reduced or cancelled outright. You'll be classified as a walk-away.

When you do decide to come back, or want an academic transcript to transfer to another school, you'll be met with a financial hold and a bill to pay before you can continue your education anywhere. Remember, you registered for your classes; you have to un-register from them if you want to withdraw in the right way. And again, talk to your academic and financial aid advisors before you take any actions. They will work with you to help you make the right decision for what you plan to do.

- **Satisfactory Academic Progress** – We're not just talking about scholarships and renewability here. This is about *all* financial aid….need-based grants, loans and part-time jobs too. In order to get your financial aid for next term or next year, the government (federal and state) requires that you have a minimum average grade ratio called a grade point average (GPA) as well as proof that you're completing or passing a minimum percentage (66.6% or 2/3) of the classes you've registered for. This is called a credit completion rate. *What is a credit completion rate?* Basically, if you attempted 30 credits, you need to have successfully earned at least 20 to 21 of those credits.

Look at it this way: The federal government is concerned about how many years they must provide financial aid for you while you're attending a two year or four year program. Remember the federal budget deficit? Well, it's still with us and growing each day. If you need four or five years to complete a two-year degree because you withdrew from classes, failed classes, repeatedly changed your major or repeated classes in pursuit of a better grade, the federal government will eventually say enough is enough.

Here's an example of what I mean.

> You and I are buddies and we're both full time students attending the same four year school in September. We are both registered for four classes (12 credits). At the end of the fall semester, you completed all four classes and earned a grade of "C" in all your classes. I took four courses but withdrew from three, and only completed one class getting a grade of "A".
>
> In the spring semester, we take four classes again and both of us end up with the same results by the end of the term. You complete your 4 classes earning a "C" grade and I complete one class and earn an "A" grade. So at the end of our first year, you passed eight classes for 24 credits and have a C average. I've completed two classes for a total of 6 credits towards my degree and have a straight "A" grade average. The college has me on the Dean's List and they're throwing ticker tape parades for me!
>
> Both you and I apply for financial aid for the next year and you qualify, but I don't. Why? How many years will you need financial aid to complete your four year bachelor's degree and graduate? Four years, perhaps five? Well, based on federal rules, that's ok. So, what about me? At the credit completion rate I'm going, I'll need seven, eight, maybe ten years to complete my four-year degree program. Does the federal or state government really want to fund me for ten years to complete a four year degree program? No way. Get it?

Every college and university in the country is required to measure a student's academic progress, GPA and credit completion rate. Each school has its own policy based on federal law that must be posted on the college's web site. Get familiar with it or contact your financial aid office and ask about it.

- **Student Loans: It's Easy to Qualify and Easy to Lose** – Once you get past the general financial aid eligibility requirements, like getting admitted to a college, being a U.S. citizen or eligible noncitizen, meeting academic progress standards, not in default (in good standing) on previous student loans, etc., anyone, *and I* *mean anyone*, can qualify and get a federal student loan. It's very easy to qualify. File the FAFSA and be enrolled in at least two classes for a minimum of six credits each semester and you're in! And, there is no application fee either!

But, here's the rub. Most colleges won't assume you want a loan so they will offer it to you and keep it in "offer status" until you tell them you want it. If you don't tell them in a timely way that you want the loan, they'll cancel it, so this is another good reason to read your mail regularly. Also, if you withdraw from one or some of your classes so that you fall below half time status (under 6 credits a semester), you will see your loan cancelled. Before you withdraw from a class, talk to your financial aid counselor.

Non-payment of previous student loans can also result in the cancellation of your current financial aid awards if you are in *default*. Defaulting on a student loan means you have not been making payments against your college student loans as promised. While you are in default, you cannot receive any federal or state financial aid. You can change your loan default status by talking to a counselor in the financial aid office or a customer service representative in the U.S. Department of Education and getting information about their loan Rehabilitation Program or you can remove the default status by participating in the Direct Loan Consolidation Program.

* * *

Chapter. 12

Scholarships:
How To Find Them For Free

Did you know that there are millions, perhaps billions of dollars in scholarships available from private and government sources? The awards range from a few hundred dollars to a full tuition and fees scholarship for four years! Full tuition and fees scholarships can be $30,000 a year or more for students working toward a four year bachelor's degree! So, how do you tap this source of apparent wealth without paying someone to find it for you?

Important: Looking for and finding scholarships is free and fairly easy, but it is also an investment in time.

Scholarships can be found based on a number of different criteria and in a number of different places. One thinks of scholarships as only being available for students based on some form of merit; academic, artistic or athletic; and certainly, millions of dollars are awarded to qualifying students based on these forms of merit every year. But merit awards are not only limited to academic over-achievers. Anyone can qualify for scholarships based on their community involvement, ethnicity or choice of academic program. Scholarships may be awarded on a "one-time" basis or can be renewed, typically over a four year period. Renewability is often based on some minimum requirement, such as a minimum grade point average (GPA), continuous attendance or minimum performance of some type. You may ask when the best time is to start looking for scholarships. The general rule of thumb is to start your search in October of your high school senior year when you are beginning your college search and reviewing your financing options (like student financial aid). But, there's no harm in beginning earlier like in your high school sophomore or junior year. The sooner you begin, the better. The key in the scholarship search process is determination and perseverance.

Essentially, scholarships are awards of free money to help cover college expenses. They are awarded to students based on meeting the donors' criteria for the award, and earning the award in competition with other qualified applicants. Academic scholarships are scholarships awarded to students for academic accomplishments or academic promise. Application selection can be based on standardized test scores, grade point average, rank in class, artistic talent, community service or leadership positions held in high school or college. Applying for these funds may come in the form of a simple application, like your college admissions application, a merit-based competition, or an essay contest. They may even require a face-to-face interview before a decision is rendered. Some colleges will offer full tuition and fees awards renewable for 4 years, but room and board expenses might not be covered. Other colleges will offer awards for less than full tuition and in varying amounts based on each scholarship student's credentials. And speaking of colleges, don't stop with your admissions application. Contact the academic department of your chosen major. They may be offering academic scholarships of their own.

How do you find scholarships?

You can research scholarships in several ways, including contacting the financial aid office at the school you plan to attend or checking information in a public library or online on various web sites. As a word of precaution, be sure scholarship information and offers you receive are legitimate by remembering that you don't have to pay a fee up front or pay any service to find scholarships or other financial aid for you. There are legitimate online scholarship databases that are free to use and are a vital component of a complete scholarship search process. For a list of these online sources, go to my web site at www.fafsafriend.com.

When you begin your search on these free scholarship sites, you'll complete a profile form asking questions about you. When you complete and submit your profile, it will run through the sites' database of scholarships on a regular basis, hunting for a scholarship program that matches the information you've included in your profile. If there are matches, you'll be notified that you are eligible to apply to the matched program. Answer as many profile questions as possible so that your list of qualifications is as complete as possible. This will increase the number of scholarship matches or "hits" produced. Do not limit your search to these online resources, exclusively. Students who search for scholarships solely through these search engines find limited success. Try these additional free sources of information about scholarships:

- The financial aid office at a college
- A high school guidance counselor
- The U.S Department of Labor free scholarship search tool, located at http://careerinfonet.org/scholarshipsearch/
- Other federal agencies, such as the U.S. Department of Education
- Your state financial aid agency or office
- Your library reference section
- Foundations, religious or community organizations, local businesses or civic groups
- Organizations related to your field of study
- Ethnicity-based organizations
- Your employer or your parents employers, including unions
- Political organizations

Ok, I know where to start my search for scholarships. What do I do now? The only way to have a chance of being selected for a scholarship is to apply for scholarships. It sounds simple, but this process will demand a good amount of your time and effort to lay the foundation for your success. Here's another easy-to-remember tip; apply early, and apply often. And please, keep a watchful eye on program deadlines. Don't miss these deadlines, or you'll go to the bottom of the application pile. And don't sell yourself short; apply for scholarships even if you think that a program is a "reach" (as long as you meet the minimum qualifications). You could be missing out on an opportunity for substantial money that you won't need to pay back. Do your research and look in every nook and cranny for scholarship hideouts. As a result, you'll be prepared for your scholarship adventure, seeking out your share of the free money out there.

The Application Process

When you're ready to start applying, it's important to get organized. Once you've compiled a good list of potential scholarships, review the eligibility and application guidelines. Don't bother with scholarship programs if you clearly don't qualify. Applying to programs where you don't meet minimum requirements is a waste of your valuable time. Organize your list by assessing the value of the scholarship award and the earliest approaching deadlines. Make programs that meet your criteria your first priority. Read the directions and qualifications of each scholarship and make note of what you need to do, in what order, and within what timeframe. You will find that some tasks for any one scholarship can be applied to multiple scholarship applications – such as an essay or writing sample. If a scholarship program includes an essay as part of the application, start working on your essay as soon as possible. You can ask teachers, family or friends for initial feedback. Remember, applying for and winning scholarships is about competition, putting your best foot forward. Producing standout essays is essential for judges to notice you above the other applicants in the pool.

Here are some basic tips for writing effective essays;

- Read the instructions carefully, making sure you understand the question before you start writing.
- If you have a choice of topic, choose a theme carefully and make it personal. Admissions advisors suggest that you write about how an experience affected you and suggest how it affected your future actions as well.
- Organize your thoughts by writing an outline.
- Use clear and simple language. The key here is to communicate effectively, touching on each point you wish to make. Check and re-check your spelling and grammar. Don't rely completely on the grammar and spell-check in your word processor. Have someone proof-read it when you're done.

- Use a standard and readable font. Some scholarship programs will require a certain font and size to be used in your essay. Check the scholarship program instructions.
- Read the instructions and question again, then read your essay to make sure your essay is meeting the points in your scholarship question entirely.

An interview, particularly in cases where colleges are offering scholarship opportunities, is not an unusual requirement. Admissions or scholarship committees want to associate a face to the name on that glowing application and brilliant essay. Your scholarship is on the line so it's ok to feel nervous, but you can turn this event into a positive conversation. Keep in mind that although you are competing with other applicants, the judges are usually admissions staff or even volunteers whose job it is to identify good candidates. They are actually hoping in their hearts that you do well. In any interview, whether it's for admissions, scholarship award consideration or your first career-building job, the key to a successful interview is preparation. Keep these basic tips in mind;

- If an interviewer wants to know more about you, provide concise answers indicating your background and qualifications for the award. Don't tell your life story.
- Consider telling specific stories about your school activities or accomplishments. Judges (and most people) associate well-delivered stories as memorable and help you stand out among other candidates.
- Be informed; read a newspaper or national magazine prior to your interview and always arrive early, even by a few minutes.
- Last, dress the part and look sharp and don't forget to smile, have good eye contact and a firm handshake.

What are the sources of scholarships?

Many state governments have authorized scholarship programs for their state residents, but the majority of scholarship programs are offered by colleges and universities and by private donors and organizations.

- **State Scholarships**: Some of the most common scholarships you'll find through a scholarship search will be state scholarships, awarded directly by your college or through state-based programs. State scholarships will be merit and need-based. Merit-based awards will recognize your academic achievements in high school, such as a high grade average (GPA) and standardized test scores, while need-based scholarships look at your information and results of your processed FAFSA that will indicate your ability to pay for your college education. You can find more information about these tax-sponsored programs from the state financial aid agency or any local college financial aid office.

- **College/University Scholarships:** Many colleges and universities, all across the country, public or private, big and small, offer merit-based scholarships, as well as academic program-specific assistantships, fellowships or other scholarships. These scholarships offer one year awards, two year awards, or full tuition and fees scholarships for four years of education. Colleges often use lofty names for these institutional programs, like "Trustee" or "Presidential" scholarships. Schools will advertise the availability and details of their scholarship programs on their web site or in their admissions materials.

- Keep in mind that you do not need to be at the top of your high school class to qualify for one of these scholarships. Hardly, and this may surprise you. Colleges do not award these scholarships based solely on your talent, but to attract you to their college or academic program to fulfill one or many of their institutional goals. So for instance, a college has a new academic program being offered this coming year. To fill the seats, they award tuition scholarships to those who declare a major in this program. Or a college has a directive from their state agency to increase their student diversity, so they offer scholarships to a diverse ethnicity of students or non-resident students to address that requirement. Your talent may be an important consideration for awarding you a scholarship, but it may not be the only criteria.

Important: There can be any number of reasons why a college offers a scholarship, so apply to be considered. You never know.

- **Athletic Scholarships:** If you are looking for an athletic scholarship from the college of your choice, be aware that the NCAA (National Collegiate Athletic Association) which governs college sports also governs which schools can award athletic scholarships. A college or university must reside in the NCAA Division I or Division II institutional grouping to be allowed to award athletic money. Many student athletes and families of student athletes dream of the "full ride" athletic scholarship, but the truth is that very few athletic awards *of any kind* are available. In fact, according to the NCAA, only about 2 percent of high school athletes are awarded athletic scholarships to compete in college. Most of these awards only partially cover college costs. The NCAA limits the number of scholarship dollars a college can offer so the college athletic department may divide the funds among as many athletes as possible. Even if you are a member of the fortunate few, it's possible that your athletic scholarship may not be renewed the following year. At many colleges, an athletes' scholarship renewability is a coaches' final decision.

- Having provided some reality to this category, don't let me stop you from moving forward. Don't sit back and hope your school finds and recruits you for their athletic program. Rather, be proactive and find schools you'd like to attend and teams you'd like to play on. Apply for admissions, apply for financial aid and contact the coaching staff to see if they might be interested in having you play for their team.

- Are you looking for athletic money from a Division III school? Sorry, this won't happen....but many colleges in this division offer significant academic scholarship and grant assistance to attract student athletes and other qualified students to their campus. Many teams in the Division III pool have competitive programs in many sports. Give them a look.

- **Private Scholarships**: As discussed before, there are a number of powerful and *free* search engines on the internet to quickly match you with potential scholarship programs. But these large databases are sought on a national level, where the competition is high. There are also a number of free smaller scholarship search web sites in your geographical area that have less competition and may offer similar amounts of money for your college expenses. Many of these databases are found through your local public library, state university systems, and through your high school guidance counselor. You can also find a complete listing of free scholarship search engines on my web site, located at www.fafsafriend.com. Actually, the best place to find and win scholarships is in your hometown…your high school, clubs and civic organizations, as well as companies in your town. Contact your Chamber of Commerce, talk to community leaders, school and public librarians and your friends and neighbors. Check with the company you work for, as well as the company your parents work for; they often have tuition assistance programs for their employees and their children as well as possible scholarship programs.

So how exactly do I get the scholarship money? That depends on the scholarship. The money might go directly to your college, where it will be applied to any tuition, fees, or other amounts you owe, and then any leftover funds given to you. Or it might be sent directly to you in a check. The scholarship provider should tell you what to expect when it informs you that you've been awarded the scholarship. If not, make sure to ask.

The last word: Scholarships can be found and they are a good resource to help you pay for college. Be sure to explore this source of financial aid. A complete financial strategy that addresses college costs can include scholarships, financial aid awards from your FAFSA, college savings accounts and the use of interest-free payment plans (if necessary). Scholarships can have an impact on the financial aid you may receive from your college of choice. A scholarship will affect your other student financial aid awards because all your student aid added together can't be more than your cost of attendance at your college or university. So, you'll need to let your school know if you've been awarded a scholarship so the financial aid office can include this award in your financial aid package of awards and ensure that the total amount is not more than the cost of attendance. If it does, then an adjustment must be made. Very often, if your financial aid must be changed, it's usually your student loan award that gets reduced. That's good, right?

Keep in mind that you have multiple years of educational costs and scholarships can be one-time only awards. Granted, it would be nice if all scholarships were renewable in some way or another for every year you're in school, but that's not always the case. Some programs are renewable and some are not. Know the difference. Do your own research. You don't really need anyone to find these programs for you. The nice thing about scholarship searches is that you can do them anytime… before you enter college or while you're actually attending school. That includes graduate work too. Assistantships, fellowships and other merit awards are offered through college programs as well as private foundations and organizations.

If all this sounds too difficult, it really isn't. The process is time-consuming and you'll definitely improve your writing skills, but the investment of your time and effort will be worth it. Once you've completed an application or two, you will find that it gets easier and takes less time to compete for additional awards. Remember: you're not alone. You may feel unprepared and a tad overwhelmed at the beginning, but with a little research, organization, and a helping hand or two (like this book), you could be on your way to successfully financing your college education.

* * *

Chapter. 13

How to Save For College: The 529 Plan

I f college classes are just around the bend for you, this slice of information is definitely not for you. Instead, apply for financial aid, start a scholarship search, get a part-time job. Saving for college? Big-time too late.

However, if you're a parent or guardian and you're thinking about saving for a college education for your youngster, pre-teen or teen, then the advice here can help. The earlier you start saving, the better and the more you can spare the better. But, even the smallest regularly saved amount helps. At some point, saving for college may have little impact on the cost of a college education, but it still makes sense to start saving even when the child enters high school.

A college education is an investment in your child's future. An investment in your child's education is the best investment you can make. In a survey conducted by the U.S. Census Bureau in December 2000, it was reported that the average salary for people with a bachelor's degree was $45, 678, as compared to the $24,572 earned each year by people with only a high school diploma. A college education opens doors of opportunity that high school grads just can't take advantage of.

Figuring out how to pay for a child's college education can be one of the largest financial endeavors you'll undertake. Even today, a four year college education at a state-supported school can cost thousands of dollars each year. Considering how yearly increases to college educational expenses continually outpace annual inflation rates, you're probably thinking that this is like climbing Mt. Everest with a toothpick.

Scary, I know. Paying for college is not an easy project. This will be a challenge, but it can be done. Remember this one important point: Paying for college is best approached by strategically using different means to pay for college and involving the whole family, including your future student. There are three avenues to pay for college;

- Financial aid, including student and parent loans (loans involve future income)
- Parent and student wages (current income)
- Saving enough money to contribute or pay for college (past income)

This strategic payment approach is about tailoring all three ways so they fit your individual circumstances. You can control college expenses by choosing an affordable college as well as managing educational costs after you begin attending.

If you have time, preparing for future college expenses through savings can be an important foundation in addressing the storm of expenses coming your way. It's like having that portable radio and a bunch of batteries when the lights go out. While paying for loans uses your future income to make payments, perhaps long after your child graduates from college, monthly savings contributions use past earnings. Saving for college turns out to be less expensive monthly than the payments you'll be making for loans, so it pays to save!

How much should I save each month? Even a small monthly amount like $50 started at birth or soon thereafter can yield a substantial sum when your child is ready to cross the threshold of college. Invested wisely (that means stay away from regular savings accounts), you could find upwards of $20,000 waiting for you. Saving $200 a month could produce approximately $80,000, depending on prevailing interest rates.

Years ago, there were precious few college savings plans out there, so most families were on their own, unless they employed a financial planner who helped invest their money in higher-yield saving tools and took advantage of tax breaks. Most families just tucked some cash in a regular bank savings account and hoped for the best. Today you have better options and the best and easiest is the 529 savings plan.

A 529 college savings plan is a state-sponsored savings plan that works with selected investment management companies. The plan is an extremely safe investment. The only way you'd lose your money is if the state went bankrupt. And, in many states, incentives are provided in the form of tax deductions on your state income tax return.

In most cases, you won't be dealing with state personnel, but with the chosen investment company. Most importantly, you remain the owner of the account through the years of savings and usage. In other words, the money in this account does not belong to the child; it belongs to you and that alone parlays into substantial benefits. Here are the highlights:

- You pay no taxes on the account's earnings, but you do pay taxes on your contributions as regular income.
- You decide how much you wish to save at any time.
- If your child decides not to go to college, you can roll the account over to another family member.
- Anyone can contribute to the account.
- Anyone of any income level can qualify for this plan.
- Most states have no age limit for when the money has to be used.
- If the student gets financial aid or qualifies for an unexpected scholarship, any unused money can be withdrawn without paying any penalty (you will have to pay taxes on this money). This means that you can use the funds for non-educational purposes if you want to.

Different fees apply to 529 plans, depending on the state you live in and whether you are taking the plan through the college you attend (not all colleges offer 529 plans). You are not limited to taking the plan in your state so shop around. Before you invest in a 529 plan, you should read the plan's investment pamphlet to make sure that you understand the benefits as well as feel comfortable with any limitations of the plan.

If you think your child will attend a private school, you may want to think about the Independent 529 plan. It's designed to provide assistance for private colleges, since most state plans primarily cover public college costs.

* * *

Made in the USA
Monee, IL
27 October 2024